THE RHYS WOMAN

The Rhys Woman

Paula Le Gallez

MACMILLAN

First published 1990

Published by
THE MACMILLAN PRESS LTD
Houndmills, Basingstoke, Hampshire RG21 2XS
and London
Companies and representatives
throughout the world

Printed in Hong Kong

British Library Cataloguing in Publication Data
Le Gallez, Paula
  The Rhys woman.
  1. Fiction in English. Dominican writers. Rhys, Jean,
  1894–1979
  I. Title
  813
  ISBN 0–333–48657–9

For Arnold and Heather Le Gallez

Contents

Acknowledgements

This book is an adaptation of a PhD thesis which I wrote at the University of Exeter. I am indebted to Michael Wood, for his superb critical reading of my work, and his guidance during my time there; to David Henderson, for shepherding me through my research; to Peter Faulkner and Anthony Fothergill, for inviting me to participate in the MA seminars of 1982–3; to everybody who contributed to the 'Text and Theory' seminars of 1984–6; to Bernard Bergonzi, of the University of Warwick, for introducing me to the writings of Jean Rhys; and to Heather King and Daphne Bond, both of whom lent me a typewriter at various stages of the production of the manuscript. I also wish to thank André Deutsch Ltd, who kindly gave me permission to use copyright material from the following works of Rhys: *Tigers are Better-Looking*; *Quartet*; *After Leaving Mr Mackenzie*; *Voyage in the Dark*; *Good Morning, Midnight*; *Wide Sargasso Sea*; *Jean Rhys: Letters 1931–1966*.

Introduction

The concern of many critical theorists today reflects a movement away from the notion of the text and the writer as completed independent objects, towards the idea of reading as a process which creates the text. Philippe Sollers, quoted by one of the most acute critics of our time, Gérard Genette, aptly expresses this trend:

> Today the fundamental question no longer concerns the *writer* and the *work*, but *writing* and *reading*, and consequently it is our task to define a new space in which these two phenomena might be understood as reciprocal and simultaneous, a curved space, a medium of exchanges and reversibility in which we would at last be on the same side as our language ... Writing is linked to a space in which time would have *turned* as it were, in which there would no longer be anything but that circular, operational movement.[1]

Thus, it is the actual process of the production of the text by the reader which changes our concept of what writing is, and an awareness of this must inevitably colour any serious critical enquiry.

This book arises from a recognition that no reader-based textual analysis of the work of Jean Rhys has yet been undertaken, and that such a response is long overdue. So far, there have been only four book-length critical works on Rhys,[2] and in common with the numerous articles and reviews on her writing they have revealed four major areas of interest: the West Indian dimension, dwelt upon at length by Louis James; the feminist aspect, considered by Thomas Staley, Peter Wolfe, and particularly by Helen Nebeker; the psychological reading, exemplified by Nebeker's Jungian/ Freudian interpretation; and the autobiographical view, to which all four critics subscribe. However, in their preoccupation with content, the texture of the writing itself has largely been ignored even though Thomas Staley does go some way towards outlining Rhys's stylistic development in his effort to assess her craft as a writer and to show her relationship to 'the widely varied currents of modernism.'[3]

Dependence upon biographical information to elucidate the texts raises certain questions. Very often, this approach is made in the effort to reduce what is complex and particular in Rhys's writing to a simple formula, and to show how each novel fits into such a pattern. Although a certain amount of simplification is unavoidable in literary criticism – indeed, criticism cannot exist without it – in the case of Jean Rhys it does seem to have been taken to an extreme. A result of this is that we find many critics referring to the 'Rhys woman', an ubiquitous creature who turns up in all the novels, 'the same woman at different stages of experience'.[4] Time after time, this 'archetypal woman'[5] is depicted as a 'passive victim'[6] who is seen as being an extension of Jean Rhys's own personality. Interviewers constantly point out the similarity between the concept of this 'Rhys heroine' and the writer herself. Marcelle Bernstein, for example, one of the first to interview Rhys, makes this link explicit:

> Her life seems to have been a drifting, haphazard, emotional affair. London, Paris, Vienna, Budapest have all been her homes. Married three times, she describes herself as "passive. I'm not very much a chooser. I'm much more a being chosen. I really don't know why I've had such a restless existence." The women in her books are mirrors in which she examines herself minutely. They are passive too, soft, sad, uncertain creatures with pretty faces and a liking for liquor. Their sexual generosity is seldom repaid and their hearts and beds are left, in the end, as empty as their purses.[7]

Ned Thomas, too, finds a similarity between the writer's own remarks and those of 'a born victim'.[8]

But when we turn to Rhys's own reflections on being interviewed, given when she herself is writing an article and is not in the presence of an interviewer, we receive a different view altogether. Far from being able to accept these generalisations, she found them to be restricting, and resented being manipulated into a pre-determined part:

> The question-and-answer game goes on. I realize that I am being gently pushed into my pre-destined role, the role of victim. I have never had any good times, never laughed, never got my own back, never dared, never worn pretty clothes, never been

happy, never known wild hopes or wilder despairs. In short, I
have never been young or, if I was, I've forgotten all about it.
Wailing, I have gone from tyrant to tyrant; each letdown worse
than the last.[9]

And, in a later interview than that with Marcelle Bernstein, she
contradicts the idea of her own passivity which was put forward
then:

> I'm always being made into a victim . . . a passive person . . . but
> the fact is I was active. God knows I hardly think I should be
> copied in the way I lived my life and loves; but I didn't always
> make a mess of them, and I wasn't always the abandoned one,
> you know. My affairs ended mostly because I wanted them to
> end or I wanted to leave the place where they'd happened, or
> just wanted to get away.[10]

This reluctance to draw a parallel between her own experiences
and those of her fictional characters is aired elsewhere too. In a
letter to her daughter, she bemoans the inability of people to read
the first-person pronoun in any other way than as an indication of
the writer herself:

> . . . I would like to send you a very short story and implore you to
> type it for me.
>   It is not (repeat *not*) autobiography, and not to be taken
> seriously. But the people here are terribly narrow minded and
> they gossip like crazy . . .
>   For them "I" is "I" and not a literary device. Every *word* is
> autobiography![11]

The confusion of autobiography with fiction is most often made in
critical works on *Quartet* because parts of the novel are based on
actual events which took place in Rhys's own life. The writer
herself acknowledges this in a letter to Francis Wyndham, in which
she states that 'some of it was lived of course'.[12] But this assertion
does not excuse those critics who make a total identification of the
main character with Jean Rhys. It is quite natural to assume that
the novels are autobiographical, but the difficulty is that the
readers who do so do not concede Rhys as a writer of fiction any
freedom to maintain that the 'I' of the novels is not the 'I' which

relates to the writer herself. Furthermore, the problem is compounded by the fact that the question cannot really be settled by an appeal to Jean Rhys who may have personal reasons for denying the autobiographical nature of the text.[13] Clearly, these difficulties point towards the necessity to free Rhys's main characters from a forced relationship to the writer herself if the structures within the actual texts, structures which allow each main character to emerge individually as a fictional creation rather than as a representation of the writer's own self, are to be appreciated fully. Such an approach does not rest on the matter of protecting Rhys's privacy, but rather on the matter of reading the actual books themselves unhampered by any autobiographical angle of enquiry.

My analysis of Rhys's texts will demonstrate that the concept of the 'passive victim' – a label with which her main characters are constantly being saddled – is a more complex one than has been suggested hitherto. It will be seen that the 'Rhys woman', far from being as passive as she looks, is passive only in a culturally determined way, and that underlying this attitude is an ironic awareness that the quality is actually part of the feminine condition in the society in which she lives.

In the past twenty years or so, feminist writers have been at pains to make people more aware of the social history which accounts for the oppression of women. Kate Millett's efforts, for example, are well known. They have helped to bring about a swing away from the widely held Freudian view that 'passivity, masochism and narcissism' are natural characteristics of females, in favour of the idea that women are, in fact, 'socialized into such roles'.[14] The early short story 'Mixing Cocktails' suggests that Jean Rhys, unconsciously no doubt, did not herself sympathise with the Freudian view.[15] In the oppressive atmosphere of the British expatriate society, the little girl who is the subject of the story works hard to become 'well-behaved'. This is part of her socialisation. Rhys's novels, however, call this norm into question, exposing the very unhealthiness of such passivity.

Andrea Dworkin, another radical feminist writer, develops the idea of sado-masochism being a part of the oppression of women by men in society at large.[16] While the aim of her work is political and it is polemical in tone, the social history which she outlines in her books makes fascinating reading alongside the novels of Jean Rhys. Whereas Rhys appears to be writing from the perspective of one who is totally immersed in this oppressive system, not without irony, but certainly not with any revolutionary purpose, Dworkin, on the other hand, denounces the system with fervour and intent. I quote from her work not only because of the insight which it brings into the nature of the passivity of the sort of women whom Rhys happened to write about, but also to demonstrate that feminist critics of forty or so years later than Rhys have brought out and chosen to make an explicit focus on exactly those things which Rhys herself was writing about implicitly.

Dworkin, like Millett before her, suggests that society has developed through the domination of men:

> The male sexual model is based on a polarization of humankind into man/woman, master/slave, aggressor/victim, active/passive. This male sexual model is now many thousands of years old. The very identity of men, their civil and economic power, the forms of government that they have developed, the wars they wage, are tied *irrevocably* together. All forms of dominance and submission, whether it be man over woman, white over black, boss over worker, rich over poor, are tied *irrevocably* to the sexual identities of men and are derived from the male sexual model.[17]

Already we recognise in this quotation the major themes in Jean Rhys's work: in *Quartet* and *After Leaving Mr Mackenzie* there is the dominance of man over woman; in *Voyage in the Dark* and *Wide Sargasso Sea* this theme is coupled with that of white over black; in *Good Morning, Midnight* there is that of boss over worker, as well as rich over poor. But these themes are not separate, they overlap and merge here and there in each of the books.

It is important to emphasise that Jean Rhys's purpose is quite different from that of Dworkin and Millett. In her discussions with David Plante, Rhys made her stance as a non-feminist quite clear: 'I'm not at all for women's lib. I don't dislike women exactly, but I don't trust them. You can never tell them what you really think, because if they know what you think they'll do you down'. Plante's assessment of such an attitude brings out the unconscious nature of Rhys's writing process:

> To have argued with Jean about her opinions would have been mad: she simply would not have understood if one had said: "But Jean, don't you wonder *why* you say that about women?" In terms of psychology (she said she had never read Adler, Jung

or Freud, didn't know what they were about, and didn't want to know) or social studies . . . she never asked why her main female characters acted as they did. There is about them a great dark space in which they do not ask themselves, removing themselves from themselves to see themselves in the world in which they live: Why do I suffer?[18]

The conscious espousal of non-feminist views may account for the breadth of significance of some of Rhys's themes. They are concerned with oppression in several of its forms rather than being confined to that of women alone. Consequently, at times her sympathy may be seen to be all-embracingly human, regardless of sex, when occasionally the men in her novels are shown to suffer oppression too, albeit in a different way. Thus, the concept of the 'victim' has a cultural significance which relates as much to men as to women. Men who are oppressed also require a strategy for survival. They find it through their act of oppressing women.

The implicit nature of Rhys's feminism is interesting because it points to the potential for disharmony between a writer's conscious beliefs and the conclusions which are suggested in her novels. Because Rhys lived the oppressive patriarchal system from within, she was able to write about it from within. This explains her genuine and quite natural inability to recognise consciously her own lack of power within such a system, as her comments on being 'active' rather than 'passive' suggest. The interesting point is, however, that she and her novels seem to have reached different conclusions. Rhys's own conviction was that the way to survive in a patriarchal system of oppression was to make use of the weapons of femininity given to women by that system. Clearly, this method has nothing in common with the feminist approach, or indeed with the suggestion in the novels themselves that such a tactic is a very unsatisfactory one – Rhys's women can never win.

Dworkin continues:

As nonphallic beings, women are defined as submissive, passive, virtually inert. For all of patriarchal history, we have been defined by law, custom, and habit as inferior because of our nonphallic bodies. Our sexual definition is one of "masochistic passivity": "masochistic" because even men recognize their systematic sadism against us; "passivity" not because we are naturally passive, but because our chains are very heavy and as a result we cannot move.[19]

The point is that such 'masochistic passivity' is a learned response, and it is a quality which Jean Rhys brilliantly depicts in her novels. In seeking to explain how this behaviour is assimilated into the female psyche, Dworkin focuses on the psychology behind the fairy tales which children learn in their infancy:

> The lessons are simple and we learn them well.
>
> Men and women are different, absolute opposites.
>
> The heroic prince can never be confused with Cinderella, or Snow-white, or Sleeping Beauty. She could never do what he does at all, let alone better. . . .
>
> Where he is erect, she is supine. Where he is awake, she is asleep. Where he is active, she is passive. Where she is erect, or awake, or active, she is evil and must be destroyed. . . .
>
> There are two definitions of woman. There is the good woman. She is a victim. There is the bad woman. She must be destroyed. The good woman must be possessed. The bad woman must be killed, or punished. Both must be nullified.
>
> . . . There is the good woman. She is the victim. The posture of victimisation, the passivity of the victim demands abuse.
>
> Women strive for passivity, because women want to be good. The abuse evoked by that passivity convinces women that they are bad. . . .
>
> Even a woman who strives conscientiously for passivity sometimes does something. That she acts at all provokes abuse. The abuse provoked by that passivity convinces her that she is bad. . . .
>
> The moral of the story should, one would think, preclude a happy ending. It does not. The moral of the story is the happy ending. It tells us that happiness for a woman is to be passive, victimised, destroyed, or asleep. It tells us that happiness is for the woman who is good – inert, passive, victimised – and that a good woman is a happy woman. It tells us that the happy ending is when we are ended, when we live without our lives or not at all.[20]

Thus, the passivity, or victimisation, of the woman is seen as a 'posture', and the similarity of this assertion to a major theme in Jean Rhys's first novel, originally titled *Postures*, is quite astounding. Though Dworkin nowhere mentions Rhys, it is almost as though she had the writer's novels in mind when composing her tracts. Each of Rhys's main characters appears to suffer from precisely those symptoms which she outlines. What is most significant about this similarity is that it suggests that the 'Rhys heroine', far from being a literary construct limited in its scope, does in fact have more universal significance than critics have hitherto been inclined to allow.

A prerequisite for taking any specific approach into a writer's work, be it feminist, psychological, or even autobiographical, is to examine the language closely. In this book, I aim to move away from the type of critical reading which allows peripheral elements in the work of Rhys to be stressed at the cost of attention to the language itself. There will be no conscious effort on my part to make the novels fit into a particular pattern, for I believe that it is only after we have looked at the language with which the novels have been constructed that we should even begin to consider employing these other approaches. An implication of this strategy is that every word in every novel should be looked at and considered. Clearly, it is not possible for me to offer such a complete reading; some selection must necessarily occur. My decision to focus upon character, therefore, is made not only in the effort to adjust the oversimplification by critics who have synthesised all five major characters into one 'Rhys woman', but also to give my analysis of the language some direction. The purpose of my detailed examination of selected parts of each novel in turn is twofold. Firstly, I hope that the focus on the language itself will enable me to avoid falling into the trap of pushing the main character into her expected mould – any judgements which I make on character will be supported by textual evidence. Secondly, the fact that I treat each novel as an artistic whole, complete within itself, should allow me to appreciate the complexity of each personality and see her in terms of her own individuality. In my examination of the language, I have been influenced by Gérard Genette's analytical approach to Proust's work.[21] My adoption of some of his critical tools leads me to a deeper penetration of the texts than I would be able to achieve without it, and allows me to perceive structures of meaning which have hitherto lain unobserved by critics of Rhys's work.

I hope that the unconscious feminism of a consciously nonfeminist writer will become clear in the process of the following reading, and also that the novels of Jean Rhys will be shown to have nothing to fear from the most detailed textual analysis.

1

Reducing Fifi

Although I have chosen to make the novels the main focus of my attention in this book, no study of Jean Rhys would be complete without some recognition of her accomplishment as a writer of short stories. The text which I have selected for analysis in this chapter is 'La Grosse Fifi', which originally appeared in her first published work, the collection titled *The Left Bank*.[1] There are two reasons why I have chosen an early piece within the canon. Firstly, I wish to draw attention to the fine quality of the writing, a quality which is often overlooked by critics who tend to damn these stories with faint praise, assessing them as products of the writer's apprenticeship, and valuing them primarily as forerunners of the novels.[2] Secondly, in the process of reading 'La Grosse Fifi', I hope to demonstrate what an important bearing the story has on Rhys's feminism. Fifi's treatment both in the text and at the hands of her lover coincides with Dworkin's observation about the oppression of women in a patriarchal society. Death is the extreme form of passivity. Fifi's death is effected in the diegesis[3] through her murder. She is silenced at the point at which she tries to assert her own needs and desires. But her death is also effected in the text itself, through a gradual reduction of the character in such a way that the actual narrative, the matrix of the work, literally swallows up the personality.

The process of the reduction of Fifi is initiated on her introduction into the text. This is effected dramatically by the reaction to her of a minor character, Mark Olsen, rather than by any traditional descriptive means: '"Oh my Lord! What's that?"' The gracelessness of this response is shown up by the contrasting pleasure which Roseau, a major character in the work, demonstrates on seeing this woman:

"That's Fifi," answered Roseau in a low voice and relaxing into a smile for the first time.

9

"Fifi! Of course – it would be – Good Lord! Fifi!" His voice was awed. "She's – she's terrific, isn't she?"
"She's a dear," said Roseau unexpectedly."[4]

At this point, the irony of the narrative voice emerges in a sustained description of the centre of attention: 'Fifi was not terrific except metaphorically, but she was stout, well corseted . . .'. Here, the narrator has the visual acuity of an artist's eye. Montparnasse Impressionism, however, gives way to the Surrealistic 'stomach carefully arranged to form part of her chest', and the Expressionism not only of her rouge which 'shrieked' but also of the 'bright blue' colour of her eyelids. Such distortion of vision defamiliarises our concept of the human. It makes for a caricature of Fifi, whose head looms large on top of a diminutive body: '. . . her face looked huge – vast . . . Her small, plump hands were covered in rings, her small, plump feet encased in very high-heeled, patent leather shoes.' The certainty that this rather savage perspective belongs to the narrator and is not that of either of the two onlookers, comes with the omniscient detail of the contents of the glass: '. . . her voice was hoarse though there was nothing but Vichy water in her glass.' But an indefinite point of view returns again with the comment that 'Fifi was obvious in fact – no mistaking her mission in life.' This could quite easily be the perspective of Roseau, and the colloquial flavour of the last part of the sentence, with its omission of the main verb, suggests that it is indeed a thought impression, a moment of free indirect style.[5]

One of Roseau's functions as a main character in the text is to provide a means through which the personality of Fifi can emerge. From a narrative point of view, their relationship is symbiotic. With much of the discourse being orientated from Roseau's perspective, Fifi is dependent for her textual life on the impression she makes upon Roseau. What Roseau sees, the reader sees. For her own part, Roseau is dependent upon Fifi in the sense that the force of the story hinges on her gradual recognition that this woman is her kindred spirit.

Fifi's dependence for her textual life upon Roseau is brought out quite early in the story, when there is a lull in the action concerning the younger woman, and here we see a very subtle mingling of Roseau's role with that of the third-person narrator. Mark Olsen has just departed, leaving Roseau alone and bored for a few moments. At this point there appears to be a shift from Roseau as

the immediate focus of narrative attention, but on a closer examination, the apparently classical third-person mode may be
identified as evolving into Roseau's own impressions: 'She
finished her aperitif gloomily. She was waiting for an American
acquaintance who was calling to take her to lunch. Meanwhile, the
voices of Fifi and the gigolo grew louder.' (p.174). From a grammatical point of view, this fade-out is achieved very economically. The
first sentence, in the classical third-person tense, brings this brief
scene to an end. But the imperfect tense of the second sentence
implies that the narrator does not dispense with Roseau, and that
the cameo scene with Fifi and the gigolo which follows is what
Roseau observes as she whiles away the time. The use of 'meanwhile' acts as the refocusing device to allow the shift to the two
new characters, but also it marks a point at which it is no longer
possible to distinguish the narrator's mind from that of Roseau
herself. Now the text resumes the drama of direct speech although,
as yet, the utterances are broken up with moments of pure
narrative:

> "I tell you," said the gigolo, "that I must go to Nice this
> afternoon. It is necessary – I am forced."
> His voice was apologetic but sullen, with a hint of the bully.
> The male straining at his bonds.
> "But mon cheri," implored Fifi, "may I not come with you? We
> will take tea at the Negresco afterwards."
> The gigolo was sulkily silent. Obviously the Negresco with Fifi
> did not appeal to him. (pp.174–5)

It is the brevity of this passage which lends it the flavour of an
interlude – a momentary break from the more important business
of the text. And the fact that the narrator even chooses to break into
a sentence rather than complete it before effecting the change of
focus is the clearest sign that this short scene has formed the
content of Roseau's own thoughts while she has been waiting for
her friend to join her: '"I think so, I will see," answered the gigolo
loftily, following up his victory as all good generals should – and at
that moment Roseau's American acquaintance entered the restaurant.'

The mediating influences which control Fifi's portrait in the text
are, perhaps, best seen in the episode in which, disturbed by
Roseau's restlessness one night, she pays her a visit to check that

all is well. With the emergence of Fifi into Roseau's bedroom, the perspective shifts from the free indirect style which immediately precedes it, back to that of the external eye, and the reader is thrown again into the world of the classic realist text, where dialogue is intermingled with action in an essentially traditional form. Insufficient narrative irony in the emerging passage would give it a sentimental flavour, with Roseau collapsing into tears and Fifi doing her best to console her. However, Fifi's own look of 'comic amazement', together with the grotesque image of her in her 'transparent nightgown of a vivid rose colour trimmed with yellow lace' and the 'dirty dressing gown', keeps everything in an ironic check. Furthermore, there is something humorous about her carefully stylised speech. The narrator tells us that 'Fifi disliked foreign languages being talked in her presence' (p.179), and from her comments on Roseau's perfect understanding of French (p.80), we can assume that the pair of them speak to each other in French. Thus, the narrative rendering of Fifi's own speech patterns, half in French, half in unidiomatic English, tempers the sympathetic content of her utterances with humorous irony:

> "Ma petite," said Fifi with decision, "You will be better in bed, believe me. Where is your chemise de nuit? Ah!"
> She took it from the chair close by, looked rapidly with a calculating eye at the lace on it, then put a firm hand on Roseau's skirt to help her with the process of undressing.
> "La," she said, giving the pillow a pat, "and here is your pocket handkerchief." (p.177)

The ultimate effect of such stylisation of speech is not to create a full-blooded character such as the writer of the classic realist text strove for, but rather to create a caricature which, in a sense, takes away from the 'reality' of the individual. Gérard Genette has observed this tendency in relation to Proust's fiction. He writes:

> "Stylized" speech is the extreme form of the mimesis of speech, where the author "imitates" his character not only in the tenor of his remarks but in the hyperbolic literalness of pastiche, which is always a little more idiolectical than the authentic text, as "imitation" is always a *caricature* through accumulation and accentuation of specific characteristics. And so Legrandin or Charlus always gives the impression of imitating himself, and

finally of caricaturing himself. Here the mimetic effect is thus at its height, or more exactly at its limit: at the point where the extreme of "realism" borders on pure unreality. The narrator's unerring grandmother says rightly that Legrandin talks "a little too much like a book." In a larger sense, this risk lies heavy over any too-perfect mimesis of language, which finally annuls itself in the circularity – already noted by Plato – of the link to its shadow: Legrandin talks like Legrandin (in other words, like Proust imitating Legrandin), and speech, finally, sends one back to the text that "quotes" it (in other words, to the text that in fact constitutes it).[6]

The implications of this for the status of Fifi are significant. Roseau's reference to her as a 'ruin of a woman' (p.181), does not merely anticipate her eventual death, but it has a curious ring of literary truth. It is as though, like the Proustian character who 'finds this highly symbolic form of death: doing away with himself in his own speech',[7] she too has already done away with herself. The death here is in the narrative, and it is a different type of death from that which is effected in the diegesis and which Fifi suffers at the hands of her gigolo. The effect of this narrative death is not, however, unkind. The narrative ruins and loses Fifi just as the world does, but the reader's sympathy for her is not lost thereby. This removal of Fifi from the immediate narrative gaze is almost a form of discretion. Fifi is made up of clichés, but there is a distinct pathos within them which allows us to respond to the humanity of her personality.

Jean Rhys is constantly at pains to make clear the peculiar position which Fifi occupies, not only through the general stylisa-tion of her speech, but also through an occasional breakdown in communication between the two women. As an example of this, we can take Fifi's idiosyncratic use of vocabulary, which firstly mystifies the receiver, Roseau in this case, who responds by mystifying Fifi. The particular instance which I have in mind is the use of the word 'disembarrass'. Although this word, meaning 'to get rid of', is very common in French, it is not used in English, and Roseau demonstrates her unfamiliarity with the concept when she hesitates before repeating it. The talk is of Roseau's recent break from a lover. Fifi, of course, has guessed at the reason behind the young woman's depression:

"Then perhaps he is méchant – there are men like that – or perhaps he is trying to disembarrass himself of you."

"That's it," said Roseau. "He is trying to – disembarrass himself of me." (p.178)

Assuming that the women are speaking in French, the position here is curiously complex. What we have in the text are several layers of functioning:

1. Fifi, the sender, in the diegesis speaks French with, we assume, the occasional word in English.
2. Jean Rhys, through the narrator, translates her utterances into English with, correspondingly, the occasional word in French, for example, 'méchant'.
3. Roseau, the receiver, in the diegesis receives the message in French.
4. Simultaneously, the narratee receives the same message in English.

Thus, Fifi talks like Fifi, but here Jean Rhys's imitation of Fifi is more complex than Proust's imitation of Legrandin, because of the nature of the translation involved. The text 'quotes' Rhys's imitation, and the receiver of the text 'gets' Fifi at several removes from the original.

The ironic beauty of this kind of linguistic game is itself implicitly acknowledged by the author in the very next part of the text. It is almost as though she is very much aware of playing with these levels of communication. This time it is Roseau's turn to mystify Fifi:

"Ah!" said Fifi wisely. She leant closer. "Mon enfant," said she hoarsely, "do it first. Put him at the door with a coup de pied quelque part."

"But I haven't got a door," said Roseau in English, beginning to laugh hysterically. "No vestige of a door I haven't – no door, no house, no friends, no money, no nothing."

"Comment?" said Fifi suspiciously. She disliked foreign languages being talked in her presence. (pp.178–9)

Not only does the final sentence of this quotation act as an ironic comment on the linguistic game of the text, but it also serves to undercut Roseau's self-pity.

As we saw in an earlier quotation with the way in which Fifi eyes the lace on Roseau's nightdress, the sentimentality is not only undercut through speech, but also through direct action. The most incisive piece of comic action which is designed purely and simply to perforate the sentimentality, comes after Fifi has 'bent down to kiss' Roseau, when the narrator delivers the following paragraph:

> It seemed to Roseau the kindest, the most understanding kiss she had ever had, and comforted she watched Fifi sit on the foot of the bed and wrap her flannel dressing-gown more closely round her. Mistily she imagined that she was a child again and that this was a large, protecting person who would sit there till she slept.

The undercutting comes with the ensuing irony of 'The bed creaked violently under the lady's weight', and with Fifi's resulting tirade against the lodgings: '"Cursed bed," muttered Fifi. "Everything in this house is broken, and then the prices they charge! It is shameful . . ."'.

Fifi's death, however, is also achieved in the narrative through yet another technical move on the part of the author. Gradually, her presence is effaced from the text, and the clue to her disappearance lies in the use of ellipsis. The action of the diegesis unfolds in the narrative in a linear fashion, with the occasional ellipsis accelerating the pace here and there. The first instance of this occurs when there is a textual shift from the afternoon to later 'that night'.[8] In the remainder of the text, a series of such ellipses serves to speed up the pace of the narrative so that it moves faster and faster towards its inevitable climax, with the intervening scenes in which Fifi appears becoming progressively shorter. Thus, as the presence of Fifi is felt to dominate increasingly, her actual presence in the text diminishes. Rhys prepares us for the removal of Fifi on at least three occasions when her presence in the narrative ceases to be direct. On the first and third occasions when this occurs, Roseau's sleep is disturbed by the sound of an argument next door. Firstly:

> Next morning Roseau, with a dry tongue, a heavy head, woke to the sound of loud voices in the next room.
> Fifi arguing, grumbling, finally weeping – the gigolo who had obviously just come in, protesting, becoming surly.

"Menteur, menteur, you have been with a woman!"
"I tell you no. You make ideas for yourself."
Sobs, kisses, a reconciliation.
"Oh Lord!" said Roseau. She put the friendly sheet over her
head thinking: "I must get out of this place." (p.179)

and thirdly:

"No one," thought Roseau, awakened at four in the morning,
"could accuse Fifi of being a little mouse." Nothing of the mouse
about Fifi. (p.185)

The second occurrence of this indirect presence is most interesting,
partly because in it Fifi manages to dominate the scene without
herself uttering a single word in the narrative. This is the occasion
of Mark and Peggy Olsen's visit to Roseau in her hotel. The
passage is punctuated throughout by derogatory remarks about
Fifi's general behaviour and character:

"That dreadful creature!" said Peggy Olsen one night. "How
does she get all those men together?"
Mark laughed and said: "Take care, she's a pal of Roseau's."
(p.183)

It is also interesting, however, from a symbolic point of view. As
though to emphasise the inevitability of Fifi's actual death, there is
a startling paragraph in which she is seen as something of a ghost
already:

The electric light went out.
The thin, alert, fatigued-looking bonne brought candles. That
long drab room looked ghostly in the flickering light – one had
an oddly definite impression of something sinister and danger-
ous – all these heavy jowls and dark, close-set eyes, coarse
hands, loud, quarrelsome voices. Fifi looked sinister too with her
vital hair and ruined throat. (p.183)

Not only does the image of the 'ruined throat' brilliantly anticipate
the 'wounds in her throat' which Fifi will suffer at the hands of
Pierre Rivière, but the whole 'ghostly' atmosphere which is evoked

here serves to emphasise my point about Fifi's death being accomplished in the narrative.

The importance of this narrative death is further borne out by the way in which the narrative deals with Fifi's actual death. Almost as though the actual death is a matter of relative unimportance, the rendering of it in the text is made at several removes from the real event, through the reproduction of a report from the *Eclaireur de Nice*. Here, the personality of Fifi is at its most reduced. Even the headline serves to point out the mundane regularity of such instances of murder, as though the incident is hardly worth recording at all: 'Yet Another Drama of Jealousy'. The report itself forms a narrative analepsis[9] in the text, the actual event having taken place 'last night':

"Madame Francine Carly, aged 48, of 7 rue Notre Dame des Pleurs, Marseilles, was fatally stabbed last night at the hotel – Monte Carlo, by her lover Pierre Rivière, aged 24, of rue Madame Tours. Questioned by the police he declared that he acted in self-defence as his mistress, who was of a very jealous temperament, had attacked him with a knife when told of his approaching marriage, and threatened to blind him. When the proprietor of the hotel, alarmed by the woman's shrieks, entered the room accompanied by two policemen, Madame Carly was lying unconscious, blood streaming from the wounds in her throat. She was taken to the hospital, where she died without recovering consciousness.

"The murderer has been arrested and taken to the Dépôt." (pp.186–7)

The journalistic summary is a reductive device which serves to present the facts as economically as possible. Thus, the Fifi whom we learnt to recognise from her stylised speech patterns, has disappeared from the text at this point. The ultimate reduction here is achieved in the use of narratised speech which indirectly reveals that she 'threatened to blind' Pierre Rivière. But this is not a question simply of narrated speech at a single remove. It is not merely Rivière who reports Fifi's words to a listener. Close textual analysis will demonstrate the many levels of reduction which operate between the actual event of Fifi's death and the presentation of it in the narrative:

Stage	Content	Level
1	Fifi is murdered by Rivière.	Action
2	Rivière describes the incident to the police.	1st narr.
3	The police inform the journalist.	2nd narr.
4	The journalist writes the article.	3rd narr.
5	The newspaper prints the article.	3rd narr.
6	Roseau reads the article.	3rd narr. received.

Over and above this, of course, we have the author, the original sender, who generates the whole process, and the reader, the ultimate receiver, who completes it, by which time the initial action has entered a fourth narrative level, that of the book.

Given that these many narrative levels obtain, it is hardly surprising that Roseau feels 'so little regret' on learning of the death of her friend. Her absence of regret does not necessarily imply that she feels a complete lack of emotion about Fifi's murder, but the confirmation of the death serves, rather, to exorcise the ghost which has been troubling her for some time: '"I must leave this hotel," was her only thought, and she slept soundly that night without fear of ghosts.' It is almost as though Fifi, who from the very beginning has been 'doing away with [herself] in [her] own speech',[10] is now at last allowed to lie to rest, the irony, of course, being that her actual death comes as something of an anticlimax.

It is remarkable that such a reductive treatment of Fifi, combined with the tendency towards caricature which we noticed earlier, does not result in the creation of superficiality. Yet the overall effect which is achieved is, rather, one of poignancy. Jean Rhys achieves this not only through the pathos within the clichés which go to make up her character, but also through the medium of poetry. Ironically, it is Fifi who sees the beauty in it, and she is the one who reads it to Roseau:

> "I adore poetry," said Fifi with sentiment. "Besides, this is very beautiful. You understand French perfectly? Then listen."
> She began to read:

> > "Dans le chemin libre de mes années
> > Je marchais fière et je me suis arrêtée . . ." (p.180)

But while Rhys gives the floor to Fifi with one hand, she takes it away with the other. There seems almost to be some sort of narrative conspiracy against Fifi. Her reading in French is interspersed with lines in English and with moments of free indirect style in which Roseau makes an impromptu translation of the poetry which her friend quotes. The result is a curiously moving narrative counterpointing which balances French and English lyricism while reminding us that the sentiments expressed are of universal significance. The conspiracy, therefore, is of necessity. Clearly, Fifi without recourse to poetry could not attain to such lyrical heights:

> "Thou hast bound my ankles with silken cords.
>
> .   .   .
>
> "Que j'oublie les mots qui ne disent pas mon amour,
>   Les gestes qui ne doivent pas t'enlacer,
>   Que l'horizon se ferme à ton sourire . . .
>
> .   .   .
>
> "Mais je t'en conjure, ô Sylvius, comme la plus humble
>   des choses qui ont une place dans ta maison – garde-moi."

In other words: you won't be rotten – now. Will you, will you? I'll do anything you like, but be kind to me, won't you, won't you? Not that it didn't sound better in French.
"Now," read Fifi,

> "I can walk lightly for I have laid my life in the hands
>   of my lover.
>
> .   .   .
>
> "Chante, chante ma vie, aux mains de mon amant!"
>
> .   .   .

And so on, and so on. (pp.180–1)

Roseau's recognition that Fifi is her own alter ego troubles her: 'Roseau thought that it was horrible to hear this ruin of a woman voicing all her own moods, all her own thoughts. Horrible.' But this dimension partly explains why the effect of poignancy is possible. Fifi, seen alone, seems grotesque, but when she is seen as an extension of Roseau's own character, then the potential for poignancy is opened up. The implication is that Roseau, herself, is a Fifi-in-the-making. It is a thought which the younger woman is reluctant to contemplate:

> "Sylvius, que feras-tu à travers les jours de cet
> être que t'abandonne sa faiblesse?
> Il peut vivre d'une sourire, mourir d'une parole.
> Sylvius, qu'en feras-tu?"

"Have you got any detective stories?" Roseau interrupted suddenly. She felt that she could not bear any more. (p.181)

Thus, the spell is broken with a return to the familiar caricature: 'Fifi was surprised but obliging. Yes – she had Arsène Lupin, several of Gaston Leroux; also she had "Shaerlock 'Olmes"', and Roseau finds some relief in equating the pastoral lyricism of the poetry with the down-to-earth sordidness of Fifi's daily life. In a spirit of flippancy, the narrator notes: 'That afternoon Roseau met Sylvius, *alias* the gigolo, in the garden of the hotel.' Yet the poignancy returns finally, when Roseau, after learning of Fifi's death, is moved to tears on rereading the poem:

> "Maintenant je puis marcher légère,
> J'ai mis toute ma vie aux mains de mon amant.
> Chante, chante ma vie aux mains de mon amant." (p.187)

This is the supreme moment of recognition. At last, Roseau is able to look at the link between herself and Fifi, and the tears which she sheds are not only for the death of her friend but also for the realisation that she, too, is at the mercy of her 'amant'. Just as Fifi has done throughout her life, Roseau will find another 'nail' to drive out the previous one, when the pain of her last relationship will be replaced by a new pain. Such a disquieting prospect must account for the bitterness of her tears 'in that disordered room' which is symbolic of the unfairness of it all.

And yet, there is a self-consciousness in the resignation with which Roseau ultimately accepts her lot. This is brought out clearly in the excellent final lines which create the impression that her acceptance is a posture:

> Till, in the yellow sunshine that streamed into the room, she
> imagined that she saw her friend's gay and childlike soul, freed

from its gross body, mocking her gently for her sentimental tears.

"Oh well!" said Roseau.

She dried her eyes and went on with her packing.

The masochism of the posture is brought out well in the feeling which is conveyed that here we see Roseau imitating herself accepting her lot.

In 'La Grosse Fifi' the degree of self-consciousness demonstrated in Roseau's attitude is an important part of what makes for the feminist stance of the text. So too is the intimate relationship between Roseau and the third-person narrative voice, which is seen in the occasional mingling of their thoughts. I should now like to turn to Rhys's first novel, *Quartet*, in which a link between the irony of the narrative voice and the perspective of the main character, Marya, becomes even more distinct.

2
Marya's Irony

A myth that the personality of the 'Rhys woman' is one of innocence seems to have become assimilated by generations of critics. Where *Quartet* is concerned, the dependence upon this myth has led to a misreading of the central character, Marya, who is constantly being seen not only as 'basically a passive creature ... a victim',[1] but even as 'a heroine totally innocent of bourgeois values and institutions'.[2] In my own reading of the novel I aim to show that there is, within the narrative voice, a level of irony which has not yet been fully perceived by critics, and which is determined by Marya's point of view. Furthermore, I suggest that there is sufficient textual evidence to make a total identification of the narrative stance with that of Marya's perspective, and that, apart from one or two omniscient forays into the thoughts of other characters, there is no other mind at work which is identifiably different from her own.

A detailed analysis of the opening chapter[3] will not only introduce us to all four of the characters who make up the 'quartet', but it will also demonstrate the emergence of a personality within the narrative voice.

As we saw in the previous chapter, the third-person narrative stance is used by Rhys in a way which effects a lessening of the traditional distance between the narrative voice and the thoughts of the main character. In the initial paragraph of this novel, too, the narrative eye declines to be classically omniscient, in favour of displaying a mixture of exactness and vagueness:

> It was about half-past five on an October afternoon when Marya Zelli came out of the Café Lavenue, which is a dignified and comparatively expensive establishment on the Boulevard du Montparnasse. She had been sitting there for nearly an hour and a half, and during that time she had drunk two glasses of black coffee, smoked six caporal cigarettes and read the week's *Candide*. (p.7)

The uncertainty of the time, suggested in 'about', is at odds with the almost obsessive listing of the precise number of coffees and cigarettes. But most perplexing of all is the use of the word 'comparatively'. This presupposes a knowledge on the part of the reader which Barthes would term an appeal to the cultural code.[4] When such an appeal is used in the work of writers within the classic realist tradition – George Eliot, for example – the reader knows what is meant; there is an accepted, generalised view which makes for a common understanding between the narrator and the reader. Where Jean Rhys is concerned, however, a social fragmentation of the codes obstructs that understanding. As yet, we are not quite sure where she stands, and consequently the appeal, as it is used here, draws attention to the point of view which determines the narrative perspective.

As if to deny that there is an indeterminacy in the focalisation, the second paragraph reverts to a far more traditional rendering of character:

> Marya was a blonde girl, not very tall, slender-waisted. Her face was short, high cheek-boned, full-lipped; her long eyes slanted upwards towards the temples and were gentle and oddly remote in expression. Often on the Boulevards St Michel and Montparnasse shabby youths would glide up to her and address her hopefully in unknown and spitting tongues. When they were very shabby she would smile in a distant manner and answer in English:
> "I'm very sorry; I don't understand what you are saying."

Thus, the diegesis, begun in the first paragraph with the detail about Marya emerging from the café, is halted in these lines while the narrator resumes the distance necessary to evoke such an external portrait. During this pause in the action, the reader appreciates a pleasing sense of balance in the narrative, which depends for its effect upon an interplay between a complex triple arrangement in the first two sentences, and a simpler dual development in the last two sentences. The compound nature of the second of these four sentences gives the effect of two sentences rather than just one, and thus the triple effect of the whole is added to by the presence of three utterances of roughly equal length:

FP	1st Feature	2nd Feature	3rd Feature
1. Marya [was]	a blonde girl	not very tall	slender-waisted
2. Her face		high cheek-	
[was]	short	boned	full-lipped;
her long	slanted up-		[and] oddly
eyes	wards towards	[and were]	remote in
	the temples	gentle	expression

Key: 1: Sentence One. 2: Sentence Two. *FP*: Focal Point.

In the analysis it may be seen that our focus is gradually narrowed, from a general outline to more distinct features of the face, before it culminates on one detail – the eyes. Such observable physical details are rarely given in Rhys's later works where the first-person narrative position, as she uses it, makes for an entirely different perspective.

A similar narrowing of focus occurs in the last part of the paragraph, where the second of the two remaining sentences qualifies and develops the thought from a general statement about the 'shabby youths' to a slightly more qualified, though still general statement about the 'very shabby'. Thus, the slowing down of the narrative pace with the physical description of Marya ends with this rather sudden introduction of an iterative[5] section in the same paragraph. Introduced into the text by the word 'Often', this is where several occurrences in the diegesis, concerning the way in which Marya interrelates with the 'shabby youths', are synthesised into one descriptive utterance. This economical mode of representation, where the differences between each occurrence are ignored in favour of the similarities, is in direct contrast to the detailed study of Marya's personal appearance. Coupled as they are in the same paragraph, it makes for a curious tempo.

Concern for narrative economy allows the introduction to a new character to occur dramatically with direct speech, and the physical description of her to emerge incidentally in the course of a sentence as it contributes to the diegesis. Thus, there is no significant narrative pause here as there was earlier: 'Miss Esther De Solla, tall, gaunt, broad-shouldered, stood looking downwards at her with a protective expression.' (p.7). A contrast is, therefore, immediately set up between the two women, and there is a distinct sexual ambiguity in De Solla's own physical aspect. When a descriptive pause does occur, however, it is followed by a neat return to the diegesis, at which point we realise that the description which we have just read is not mere 'background' information on Esther De Solla's accommodation, but it is actually what Marya observes and learns as she is taken there:

> Miss De Solla, who was a painter and ascetic to the point of fanaticism, lived in a street at the back of the Lion de Belfort. Her studio was hidden behind a grim building where the housewives of the neighbourhood came to wash their clothes. It was a peaceful place, white-walled, smelling strongly of decayed vegetables. The artist explained that a *marchande des quatre saisons* kept her stock in the courtyard, and that as the woman was the concierge's sister-in-law, complaints were useless.
>
> "Though the smell's pretty awful sometimes. Sit near the stove. It's cold today." (p.8)

This pause in the diegesis is interesting. The action is again halted while the narrator focuses on the character of the studio. But the neatness alluded to above, is achieved through a particular device. At the end of the description of the smell of the studio, Miss De Solla's own words are incorporated into the fabric of the narrative itself, when her utterance is broken up into a moment of transposed speech before being followed by completion in direct speech. Such an arrangement whereby De Solla's utterance can commence with 'Though', gives an effect of continuity between a lost moment of action and the resumption of the diegesis with these words. A narrative ellipsis has actually taken place here, in which the narrator has omitted to render a portion of the action from the moment when the two women were standing outside the shop window, to their presence inside the studio, which is indicated by the words: 'Sit near the stove'. In effect, a temporal discordance has occurred within the text with, on the one hand, the narrator slowing down the narrative tempo with the description of the studio, while, on the other hand, accelerating the pace of the action through the ellipsis.

The diegesis continues with a singulative narrative[6] of events dominated by the conversation between the two women which is directly rendered. In the ensuing discussion, Hugh Heidler and Stephan Zelli, two more of the main characters, are introduced into the text, but indirectly, through the conversation. On each occasion it is the minor character, Miss De Solla, who brings them up. In discussing a Hungarian artist whose work she shows Marya, Esther De Solla explains that he is 'a discovery of Heidler's'.

> "... You know Heidler, the English picture-dealer man, of course."
> Marya answered: "I don't know any of the English people in Paris."
> "Don't you?" said Miss De Solla, shocked. Then she added hastily, "How perfectly lovely for you!"
> "D'you think so?" asked Marya dubiously.
> Miss De Solla assured her that it was.
> "I do think that one ought to make an effort to get away from the Anglo-Saxons in Paris, or what on earth is the good of being here at all? And it isn't an easy thing to do, either. Not easy for a woman, anyhow. But, of course, your husband's French, isn't he?"
> "No," said Marya. "He's a Pole."
> The other looked across at her and thought: "Is she really married to the Zelli man, I wonder? She's a decorative little person – decorative, but strangely pathetic. I must get her to sit for me."

Here, in a short verbal exchange, the reader is introduced to two of the most significant characters in the novel. This, as well as the suggestion of Heidler's importance in the Anglo-Saxon group in Paris, is achieved dramatically and mimetically, through dialogue initially rather than pure narrative. Secondarily, however, owing to a more traditional novelistic device, that of the omniscience of the narrator, Miss De Solla's reported thoughts prepare the reader for the troubled nature of the marriage between Stephan and Marya Zelli.

Marya's preoccupation with her own thoughts is the subject of the next part of the text, and in the rendering of them, Esther De Solla's argument is gradually phased out of the discourse in another ellipsis:

> She began to argue that there was something unreal about most English people.
> "They touch life with gloves on. They're pretending about

something all the time. Pretending quite nice and decent things, of course. But still . . ."

"Everybody pretends," Marya was thinking. "French people pretend every bit as much, only about different things and not so obviously. She'll know that when she's been here as long as I have."

"As long as I have." The four years she had spent in Paris seemed to stretch into infinity.

"English people . . ." continued Miss De Solla in a dogmatic voice. (p.9)

The indirect style of the transposed speech which opens the above passage prepares the reader for the reduction of De Solla which the following part of the discourse works towards. The first ellipsis marks denote a tailing off of the direct rendering of her words when the focus is allowed to fall more fully onto Marya's thoughts. And the second set of ellipsis marks indicates the definite break in the narrative which silences the artist's 'dogmatic voice' before it has really begun. Meanwhile, the rendering of Marya's thoughts is effected directly, and the repetition of 'As long as I have' suggests the luxury of the thought process which she indulges in at this moment. This narrative licence is in direct contrast to the silencing of De Solla. Connected to this repeated phrase is a further liberating device which bears all the characteristics of free indirect style. Here, Marya's thoughts are expressed within the fabric of the narrative itself: 'The four years she had spent in Paris seemed to stretch into infinity.' In this, the lack of a declarative verb, such as – 'she was thinking' – makes for technical subtlety, in preparation, perhaps, for a later move into free indirect style. The monotonous sound of the artist's voice finds a symbolic counterpart in 'the drone of a concertina' which impinges on Marya's consciousness and leads her into a series of daydreams. The next five paragraphs are given over entirely to her thoughts, during the course of which we receive a fuller picture of her life in Paris.

The use of ellipsis marks at the end of the first two of these paragraphs not only denotes the trailing off of the thought processes but, by that very fact, it also signifies a fuller use of free indirect style which now becomes an important device in the rendering of consciousness:

The drone of a concertina sounded from the courtyard of the studio. The man was really trying to play "Yes, we have no bananas." But it was an unrecognizable version, and listening to it gave Marya the same feeling of melancholy pleasure as she had when walking along the shadowed side of one of those narrow streets full of shabby *parfumeries*, second-hand book-stalls, cheap hat-shops, bars frequented by gaily-painted ladies and loud-voiced men, midwives' premises . . .

Again, an appeal to the cultural code in 'one of those narrow streets' allows the narrator to effect collusion between the reader's own knowledge and the experience of the character. It also makes for a greater intimacy between the narrative process itself and the rendering of Marya's thought, so that they merge. The use of the second-person pronoun, a more familiar collusive device, crystal-lises this movement:

Montparnasse was full of these streets and they were often inordinately long. You could walk for hours. The Rue Vaugirard, for instance. Marya had never yet managed to reach the end of the Rue Vaugirard, which was a very respectable thoroughfare on the whole. But if you went far enough towards Grenelle and then turned down side streets . . .

The dilatory quality of the thought, seen above, for instance, in the repetition of 'the Rue Vaugirard', allows it to meander aimlessly from street to street, never achieving any real development until, as Marya becomes more deeply distracted, such vagueness gives way to a particular memory. In an analepsis, the extent of which remains external to that of the first narrative, she remembers the scene in a bar frequented by homosexuals which she had chanced upon on the previous day:

Only the day before she had discovered, in this way, a most attractive restaurant. There was no *patronne*, but the *patron* was beautifully made up. Crimson was where crimson should be, and rose-colour where rose-colour. He talked with a lisp. The room was full of men who bawled intimacies at each other; a gramophone played without ceasing; a beautiful white dog under the counter, which everybody called Zaza and threw bones to, barked madly.

There is something remarkably pure in this passage. Without seeking to pollute the discourse with moral judgement, the narrator allows the character of this Parisian gay bar to emerge in the text quite clearly, by rendering exactly those impressions which Marya experienced. Marya's own judgements are positive. The restaurant is 'most attractive', and although the use of the word 'but' draws attention to the fact that the patron is 'beautifully made up', the irony is not unkind. An atmosphere of laughter, fun and colour makes a strong contrast to the shabbiness of the streets, and the positiveness of the impression contributes to a feeling of frustration which is conveyed in the next paragraph:

> But Stephan objected with violence to these wanderings in sordid streets. And though Marya considered that he was extremely inconsistent, she generally gave way to his inconsistencies and spent hours alone in the bedroom of the Hôtel de l'Univers. Not that she objected to solitude. Quite the contrary. She had books, thank Heaven, quantities of books. All sorts of books. (pp.9–10)

Thus, Marya's feelings of 'melancholy pleasure' are thwarted by her husband's opposition, and we are given a clearer insight into the incompatibility of the pair. Where Marya sees delight, Stephan sees only sordidness. However, such inequality in the marriage does not in this case, make for tragedy or pathos. The insistence with which Marya praises her access to 'books' rings false, serving rather to render slightly comic the disappointment which she feels in being barred from her solitary walks among 'gaily-painted ladies and loud-voiced men'. The irony in those images, together with that in the name of the hotel, adds to this comic perspective, and Marya's own judgement of her husband's inconsistencies, as well as her studied resignation to them, are, again, troublesome. There is something not quite right about the violence with which Stephan objects.

The irony continues:

> Still, there were moments when she realized that her existence, though delightful, was haphazard. It lacked, as it were, solidity; it lacked the necessary fixed bacground. A bedroom, balcony and *cabinet de toilette* in a cheap Montmartre hotel cannot possibly be called a solid background. (p.10)

and there is little doubt that the point of view still belongs to Marya in the final comment which brings these passages of reverie to an end: 'Miss De Solla, who had by this time pretty well exhausted her fascinating subject, stopped talking.' This heralds a return to the diegesis which had been suspended earlier, ironically enough, the end of the 'talking' signifying a return to the talking in the narrative. Marya is the first to break the textual silence, and, in doing so, she sets a train of action in motion:

> Marya said: "Yes, but it's pretty lonely, not knowing any English people."
> "Well," Miss De Solla answered, "if that's what you're pining for. What are you doing this evening? Come along to Lefranc's and meet the Heidlers. You must have heard of Heidler."
> "Never."
> "Hugh Heidler?" protested Miss De Solla.

With this second mention of Heidler, the Barthesian mechanism of enigma is set in motion. There is melodrama in Miss De Solla's conversation at this point, and it does not go unnoticed by the narrator who, with the restricted though ironic viewpoint which we have by now come to recognise, commences her speech by transposing it with unmistakable undercutting:

> She proceeded to explain Mr Heidler, who was a very important person in his way, it seemed. He made discoveries; he helped the young men, he had a flair.
> "I believe they intend to settle in France for good now – Provence for the winter and Montparnasse for the rest of the year – you know the sort of thing. He's had a kind of nervous breakdown. Of course people say –"
> Miss De Solla stopped.
> "I like Mrs Heidler anyway; she's a very sensible woman; no nonsense there. She's one of the few people in Montparnasse whom I do like. Most of them . . . But abuse isn't any good, and it's better to be clean than kind."
> "Much better!" agreed Marya.

Marya's laconic though decisive agreement is far too clipped to be anything but ironic in tone. Nevertheless, Miss De Solla is undeterred by it, and continues by condemning the Montparnasse artists further before adding a little to her outline of Mrs Heidler. Thus, thanks again to Esther De Solla, the fourth remaining major character has been introduced into the text:

> "Not that they are mad on baths or nailbrushes, either," said the other. "Never mind." She got up and lit a cigarette. "Mrs Heidler paints, too. It's pretty awful to think of the hundreds of women round here painting away, and all that, isn't it?"

The narrator does, however, extend a little generosity to De Solla in the pathos with which the struggle of the artist is emphasised: 'She looked round her austere studio, and the Jewess's hunger for the softness and warmth of life was naked in her eyes.' But the feeling is soon dispelled when this first section of narrative ends on a distinct note of irony. Here, the moralising attitude of De Solla towards the hardships of other artists is undercut through a suggestion of the mediocrity of her own work. This is effected comically, through a farcical ritual necessitated by something as simple as extinguishing the light:

> "... Wait a minute, I've got to stand on a chair to put my gas out. My shark of a landlady won't put in electric light. Mind you, I'm fond of this place, though the smell is really awful sometimes. That head over there doesn't look so bad in this light, does it?" said Miss De Solla, wistfully. (p.11)

The final sentence brings us back to an earlier moment of ambiguity when Marya was only able to appreciate the pictures she was shown when 'helped by the alcohol'.[7]

In the second section, Marya's ironic view of things is again allowed to emerge, giving her a world-weariness and, concomitantly, showing her to be less 'innocent' than critics have suggested. The past-tense narrative of the previous section gives way to simultaneity for two paragraphs, during which a fascinating effect of stasis is achieved:

> Lefranc's is a small restaurant half-way up the Boulevard du Montparnasse. It is much frequented by the Anglo-Saxons of the quarter, and by a meagre sprinkling of Scandinavians and Dutch.
>
> The *patron* is provincial and affable. The *patronne*, who sits

beaming behind the counter, possesses a mildly robust expression and the figure and coiffure of the nineties; her waist goes in, her hips come out, her long black hair is coiled into a smooth bun on the top of her round head. She is very restful to the tired eye.

This narrative time warp momentarily shows the novel to be operating on two different temporal scales – all the action occurs in the past, but here is a moment in the work when there is perfect temporal concordance between the action and the time of the narrative. Having said that, however, very little action takes place in these two paragraphs. Apart from the patron being 'affable', and his wife sitting 'beaming' at the clients, there is no development. Indeed, the whole has the effect of a cameo, and, appropriately enough, with the words 'very restful to the tired eye', there is a suggestion that the scene is depicted from the point of view of an art lover. Is this, then, Hugh Heidler's perception? He is, after all, the 'English picture-dealer', and Lefranc's is his haunt. Have we, in these two paragraphs, come upon Heidler at a point after all the action of the novel has finished? If so, then his present is shown to be very similar to his past. Unlike Marya, whose life is in pieces at the end of the diegesis, Heidler survives with little or no damage done to his life style. Indeed, the most that he can be said to have suffered is a 'tired eye'. And yet, is there not something just a little too ironic in the assertion 'very restful to the tired eye'? There is room for hesitation here regarding the perspective of this scene, because the signs are not unequivocal. But it does make more sense to see the point of view as Marya's.

With the switch back to the first narrative level, the focus falls on the Heidlers 'sitting at a table at the end of the room'. Again, the narrative voice is not objective, for no answer to Mrs Heidler's 'Good evening' is referred to, although undoubtedly such social niceties are observed. Similarly, the introductions which Miss De Solla must make are omitted from the discourse. Such narrative selectivity is in keeping with the first impressions created on the mind of the receiver. In fact, Marya's attention is so taken up with the Heidlers that both her own and De Solla's physical presence remain invisible in the text until a little later. The reader assumes their presence only from the information given in the first section, together with other indicators such as Mrs Heidler's greetings, and the two extra 'vermouths-cassis' which Heidler orders.

Marya's initial impressions are remarkably acute. Mrs Heidler's voice is that of 'a well-educated young male'. The implications of this are sexually ambiguous, the word 'male' carrying greater sexual connotations than 'man' would have done. Although the description applies to Lois, it may be seen to suggest that her husband has homosexual inclinations; indeed, there may be ambiguity in De Solla's assertion that Heidler 'helped the young men'.[8] Perhaps, believing her husband to be attracted by such characteristics, Mrs Heidler's cultivation of the 'male' qualities in her voice is a deliberate effort on her part to keep his weakening interest from disappearing altogether. Nevertheless, being 'well-educated', she does her best to retain an expression which is 'non-committal'.

Similar efforts to hide his true nature are observed in the portrait of Heidler:

> They were fresh, sturdy people. Mr Heidler, indeed, was so very sturdy that it was difficult to imagine him suffering from a nervous breakdown of any kind whatever. He looked as if nothing could break him down. He was a tall, fair man of perhaps forty-five. His shoulders were tremendous, his nose arrogant, his hands short, broad and so plump that the knuckles were dimpled. The wooden expression of his face was carefully striven for. His eyes were light blue and intelligent, but with a curious underlying expression of obtuseness – even of brutality. (pp.11–12)

These impressions are crowned by Marya's own thought which immediately follows this description and which is in ironic harmony with the assessment given above: '"I expect he's awfully fussy," thought Marya.' The fact that she should notice the arrogance and brutality of his face on a first meeting, again suggests her own astuteness and lack of innocence.

In the complementary description of Mrs Heidler, the narrator again draws attention to the tiresomeness of Miss De Solla whose presence, although dominating the diegesis – she has been holding forth on her pet topic 'the dearth of studios' all this time – has been completely ignored in the narrative:

> Mrs Heidler was a good deal younger than her husband, plump and dark, county with a careful dash of Chelsea, and wore with assurance a drooping felt hat which entirely hid the upper part of her face. She sat in silence for some time listening

to Miss De Solla's conversation about the dearth of studios, and
then suddenly remarked to Marya:

"H.J. and I have quite made up our minds that eating is the
greatest pleasure in life. Well, I mean, it is, isn't it? At any rate,
it's one of the few pleasures that never lets you down." (p.12)

Such an arrogant change of subject has a cruelly comic effect. The
bore, De Solla, has served her purpose. She has made the introductions and she may now disappear from the narrative. That the
focus falls on these two new characters, in two descriptive pauses,
while we understand the diegesis to rattle on on an invisible plain,
prepares for the total reduction of this minor character.

In the meantime, Mrs Heidler's studied arrogance, the affectation of her pose noted in the '*careful* dash of Chelsea' (my italics),
together with the symbolism of the hat with its function to conceal,
makes for an enigmatic portrait. Just as Marya had noticed the
brutality in Heidler's eyes, so, in a balancing observation, she sees
that 'Her eyes were beautiful, clearly brown, the long lashes
curving upwards, but there was a suspicious, almost a deadened
look in them.' The combination of attractiveness and repulsiveness
complements those qualities found in her husband. And Marya's
comic view of them again gives the lie to those critics who insist on
her innocence:

"I'm a well-behaved young woman," they said, "and you're
not going to catch me out, so don't think it." Or perhaps,
thought Marya, she's just thoroughly enjoying her pilaff.

The function of 'Or perhaps' as a conjunction which connects the
first part of the quotation to the second, serves the purpose of
making explicit the link between these ironic assessments and
Marya's own thoughts. That Marya. herself, is not included in the
discussion on 'eating, cooking', and 'England', may account for the
omission of the conversation from the narrative. Its content is
alluded to in a reported summary in which Miss De Solla, at her
most reduced and under the ironic eye of the narrator, makes her
penultimate appearance in the text in a speech which is narratized,
not direct:

Miss De Solla, looking more ascetic than ever, agreed that
eating was jolly. They discussed eating, cooking, England and,

finally, Marya, whom they spoke of in the third-person as if she were a strange animal or at any rate a strayed animal – one not quite of the fold.

With this section begins a sequence of animal imagery which will be developed in the novel. Here, the implication is that Marya bears all the qualities of a displaced sheep, doomed to follow the leader, but never quite making it into the group. Exactly what the brute will make of such meekness remains to be seen, but the use of imagery does link Heidler to Marya, with the suggestion of great inequality in the coupling and the vulnerability of the latter.

Between the second and third sections, there is another ellipsis which accelerates the pace of the text so that we next meet the party as they walk away from Lefranc's. The purpose of this section is to put the relationship between Marya and Heidler in motion. The focus immediately falls onto the two of them as they walk side by side along the boulevard. They have become separated from Lois and Miss De Solla, each of whom will occupy a subordinate role in this section.

The enigmatic portrait of Mrs Heidler which was begun in the previous section is fleshed out a little further here. Marya's curiosity has been aroused, and as they sit on a terrace, drinking coffee and liqueurs, she studies the woman's features more closely. What she sees is disturbing:

> A strong, dark woman, her body would be duskily solid like her face. There was something of the earth about her, something of the peasant. Her mouth was large and thick-lipped, but not insensitive, and she had an odd habit of wincing when Heidler spoke to her sharply. A tremor would screw up one side of her face so that for an instant she looked like a hurt animal. (p.13)

Vulnerability, then, is seen to extend to this woman too, and again it is suggested through the image of an animal. While, on the one hand, this insight qualifies and readjusts the initial impression of arrogance which Lois had given earlier, on the other hand, it emphasises the suggestion of brutishness about Heidler. And just as Marya is assessing this accurately, she receives confirmation of the fact through a symbolic gesture in which Heidler, regardless of his wife's presence, stakes his claim on Marya:

"I bet that man is a bit of a brute sometimes," thought Marya. And as she thought it, she felt his hand lying heavily on her knee.

An affectation of indifference to what his hand is doing is suggested by his careful study of 'the people passing on the Boulevard Montparnasse'. But Marya is not fooled, and the narrative repetition of 'his huge hand lay possessively, heavy as lead, on her knee', makes this clear. In a moment of free indirect style her attitude is clarified:

> Ridiculous sort of thing to do. Ridiculous, not frightening. Why frightening?
> She made a cautious but decided movement and the hand was withdrawn.

Throughout the episode, Marya acts as though she is in control of the situation. She knows what the gesture implies, and dismisses it as 'ridiculous'. Indeed, in the narrative rendering of it there *is* something ridiculous about the 'huge hand' with its clumsy heaviness. She knows what she has to do to bring the incident to an end. Clearly, these are neither the judgements nor the actions of an 'innocent'; they suggest, rather, the coolness of a woman of experience.

Another textual ellipsis pushes the action on, and in the fourth and final section of Chapter 1 we meet the last remaining member of the quartet – Stephen Zelli. Given that the portraits of Marya and the Heidlers have received such a traditional fullness, it is odd that by the end of this section we know nothing about Zelli's physical characteristics other than that he is thin by comparison to the 'well-fed Heidlers'. Indeed, so occupied is the narrative perspective with features of the building, that Zelli, himself is pushed into a subordinate position:

> At a little after midnight Marya got back to the Hôtel de l'Univers, Rue Cauchois. She mounted five flights of steep, uncarpeted stairs, felt her way along an unlighted passage, flung her bedroom door open and embraced her husband violently. He looked so thin after the well-fed Heidlers. (pp.13–14)

Even when Stephen speaks, the narrative does not dwell on his words or on any response Marya might make, but focuses, rather, on a detailed description of the room:

> "*Tiens, Mado,*" he said. "You're very late." The room was large and low-ceilinged, the striped wallpaper faded to inoffensiveness. A huge dark wardrobe faced a huge dark bed. The rest of the furniture shrank away into corners, battered and apologetic. A narrow door on the left led into a small, very dark dressing-room. There was no carpet on the floor. (p.14)

So animated is the imagery in this description that one might be forgiven for suspecting some sort of pathetic fallacy to be at work here. Certainly, one might expect Marya to be 'apologetic' rather than the furniture, after all it is she who is late. But the image of the scrawny husband hardly fits the idea of the wife-beater, and thus it is unlikely that the furniture which 'shrank' back 'battered' is a substitution for the treatment which Marya receives at his hands. Meekly, receiving no response to his last utterance, Zelli continues:

> "I've just this minute got back," remarked Stephan.
> Marya said: "Well, was everything all right?" And when he answered "Yes," she asked no further questions.

Now, a little more light is cast onto his character, but again, rather than a fully-rounded picture, we are given a restricted view which is determined by Marya's response to him. Indeed, the perspective reveals more about her own personality, and has the effect of obscuring Zelli even further:

> Stephan disliked being questioned and, when closely pressed, he lied. He just lied. Not plausibly or craftily, but impatiently and absent-mindedly. So Marya had long ago stopped questioning. For she was reckless, lazy, a vagabond by nature, and for the first time in her life she was very near to being happy.

This is further evidence that the characters are seen through Marya's eyes. The suggestion is that Stephan's lack of substance in the text is a comment both on the nature of their relationship, and also on what Marya is seeing at this point. Her boredom with her husband determines his slight appearance in the discourse here, for, as with Roseau, what Marya sees – the reader sees.

The portrait of Stephan Zelli is not fleshed out until, in Chapter 2, in an analepsis in which Marya's memories of an earlier part of her life are the subject-matter, it is appropriate that her first impressions of him should be presented. These, in turn, lead logically to an account of their life together, and it is here, in the final part of the chapter, that we begin to understand the difficulties of the marriage. Stephan's uncommunicativeness forces Marya in on herself, and this is reflected textually in the last section of this chapter, where the narrative makes inroads into the woman's consciousness at such times as her full understanding of the situation is prevented by her husband's reticence. The first instance of this occurs at the end of the opening paragraph, when the narrative level shifts from the traditional reported speech of the third-person, to a direct rendering of fragments of conversations which Marya has heard but not entirely comprehended:

> Stephan had lived in Montmartre for fifteen years, he told her, but he had no intimate friends and very few acquaintances. Sometimes he took her with him to some obscure café where he would meet an odd-looking old man or a very smartly-dressed young one. She would sit in the musty-smelling half-light sipping iced beer and listening to long, rapid jabberings: *"La Vierge au coussin vert – Première version – Authentique – Documents – Collier de l'Impératrice Eugénie ..."* (p.18)

That Stephan has managed to live in Paris for fifteen years without making either friends or acquaintances comes as no surprise. The vague description of the café – we are told only that it is 'obscure' – together with the anonymous men – 'an odd-looking old man', 'a very smartly-dressed young one' – add to our impression of Zelli's underhand business deals, and this is borne out too by the detail of the 'half-light'. In such conditions, and in a language different from her own, Marya cannot hope to make sense of the 'rapid jabberings'. Instead, and as if to emphasise more directly her lack of understanding, the level of the narrative shifts so that the key words which she has managed to pick up are directly conveyed, still in the foreign language in which they were originally uttered.

A further shift in the narrative level opens the second paragraph. Here, the subject of the Empress's necklace is continued, although a translation into English has now taken place:

"An amethyst necklace, the stones as big as a calf's eye and set in gold. The pendant pear-shaped, the size of a pigeon's egg. The necklace is strung on a fine gold chain and set with pearls of an extraordinary purity." The whole to be hung as quickly as possible round the neck of Mrs Buckell A. Butcher of something-or-the-other, Pa, or of any lady willing to put up with an old-fashioned piece of jewellery, because *impératrice* is a fine word and even empress isn't so bad.

The inverted commas enclosing the first three sentences must indicate either direct speech or a quotation. That such an itemisation and description of jewellery continues the subject of discussion of the two men is not in doubt. However, the translation into English here raises the question of responsibility for the utterance. Is it merely that the narrator translates the conversation for the benefit of the reader? Or, does Marya, bored and unable to keep up with the 'jabbering', imitate the style of her husband and his associate before puncturing that imitation with the unmistakable irony of the free indirect style in the last part of the paragraph? Another interesting episode, which tends to confirm the latter view, occurs a little later, in an anecdote about Napoleon's sabre:

One evening she had come home to find Napoleon's sabre lying naked and astonishing on her bed by the side of its cedar-wood case.
("Oui, parfaitement," said Stephan. "Napoleon's sabre.")
One of his sabres, she supposed. He must have had several of them, of course. A man like Napoleon. Lots. (p.19)

Again, we notice that Stephan's utterance is rendered in the text in French. This emphasises the lack of concord between the two of them, and possibly adds a little to our impression of his secretiveness. The bracketing of his words suggests that they are incidental to the development, and this reduces his importance in the narrative. Marya's undercutting of the value he puts on this particular antique is rendered in free indirect style, which now becomes an indication of her own introspection – a further example of the lack of communication between them.

Marya's withdrawal into lone contemplation is brought out at the end of the chapter in a description of the view available from the balcony of the Paris flat:

From the balcony Marya could see one side of the Place
Blanche. Opposite, the Rue Lepic mounted upwards to the rustic
heights of Montmartre. It was astonishing how significant,
coherent and understandable it all became after a glass of wine
on an empty stomach.

The lights winking up at a pallid moon, the slender painted
ladies, the wings of the Moulin Rouge, the smell of petrol and
perfume and cooking.

The Place Blanche, Paris. Life itself. One realized all sorts of
things. The value of an illusion, for instance, and that the
shadow can be more important than the substance. All sorts of
things. (pp.20–1)

If such conclusions seem to be rather mature for the 'innocent'
Marya, perhaps their presence here, at the beginning of the novel,
emphasises the retrospective nature of the entire text. Although
Marya can behave in the diegesis in a mature fashion – we have
already seen this in her response to H.J.'s hand on her knee – there
are times when her youthful immaturity gets the better of her. The
way in which she allows herself to be manipulated by the Heidlers
is a good example of this. Occasionally, therefore, the irony which
we have attributed to her seems out of keeping with the way she
acts. It is almost as if a tension is created between the way in which
the youthful Marya feels and behaves, and the interpretation put
upon that aspect by an older, more experienced voice. Our
identification of that voice with the central character implies that
the narrative has been constructed by an older, wiser Marya, more
hardened by the very experiences which she recalls.

The discrepancy between the two levels of maturity – of the
youthful Marya on the one hand, and the more mature narrative
voice, on the other – can be sensed, however, not only in the irony,
but also in certain moments of description, when a poetic intensity
is achieved within the discourse. A good example of this is seen in
the descriptive pause which occupies a textual ellipsis between
Marya's decision to ask Esther De Solla for help following her
discovery of Stephan's arrest, and her emergence from the Métro
en route to the studio. Here, the narrator's atmospheric picture of
the rain-soaked streets along which Marya presumably treads, has
a far more sombre significance than the young woman could
possibly be credited with seeing at the time. Her appearance is
prepared for symbolically, in the pathetic fallacy of the description:

It was raining and the lights of the Moulin Rouge shone redly through a mist: Salle de danse, Revue.

The Grelot was illuminated. The Place Blanche, sometimes so innocently sleepy of an afternoon, was getting ready for the night's work. People hurried along cowering beneath their umbrellas, and the pavements were slippery and glistening, with pools of water here and there, sad little mirrors which the reflections of the lights tinted with a dull point of red. The trees along the Boulevard Clichy stretched ridiculously frail and naked arms to a sky without stars. (p.22)

A contrast between the potential gaiety to be found in the Paris nightclubs, and the actual misery of those who now 'cower . . . beneath . . . umbrellas' is achieved here. And a deeply touching sense of the helplessness of the human lot is conveyed, not only in that image of the scurrying people anxious to get away from the relentless elements, but also in the personification of the branches – 'ridiculously frail and naked arms' – which gesture towards infinity in an attitude of hope. The futility of this posture, which is suggested by the absence of any light in the sky, is further seen in the 'sad little mirrors' as they reflect the human comedy to an indifferent wilderness of space. The classic symbolism of mist and the colour red, signifying the atmosphere to be found in hell, is most appropriate.

And yet, Marya as a young woman, despite perhaps not being quite ready to see the world in these terms, is not all immaturity. Her struggle to control her own emotions is evidence of this. It may be seen throughout the novel, and usually manifests itself in a diversion of attention from the particular crisis of the moment to a matter of complete irrelevance. In the sense that this is a deliberate act of shutting herself off rather than allowing herself to become overwhelmed by the circumstances, it demonstrates an experienced handling of herself in heated situations. The meeting in which Stephan is introduced to the Heidlers is a good example to analyse in the respect that it shows Marya's capacity to protect herself by placing mental space between herself and what is happening to her. The potential for dramatic irony in this scene is great given that Stephan is unaware of his wife's affair with H.J., and, indeed, feels grateful to the Heidlers for their care of her during his imprisonment. The tension which Marya feels is conveyed immediately in her obsessive scrutiny of the entrance to the café:

> Almost immediately after they reached the café Marya, who had her eyes fixed on the door, saw Lois come in and look round with an expression of defiance. Heidler followed her. They came up to the table and sat down. The horrible moment of meeting was over. (p.107)

Absent from the text are the social niceties of the actual introductions. Instead, the tension is increased by a momentary shift in focus to Lois, the calmness of whose voice is belied by the nervousness of her movements: 'Lois began a smooth and tactful monologue. As she talked she fidgeted with her long necklace of huge, brownish yellow beads and watched the ex-convict with antagonism and curiosity.' The reduction of Stephan into 'the ex-convict' is undoubtedly a reflection of Marya's belief that this is how Lois views Stephan. Stephan himself is rendered from an external position throughout the section; his thoughts are never revealed. Heidler's portrait is drawn with characteristic irony. Like Lois, he displays his nervousness physically:

> Heidler had carefully arranged his face to look perfectly expressionless, but when he lit a cigarette his hand trembled. He cut Stephan's thanks short with nervousness. Silence. And then more desperate conversation about the café – how old it was, how famous it was, how ugly it was. (pp.107–8)

The tension in the diegesis is conveyed in the narrative through the very brevity of the sign 'Silence', and the obsessive piling up of the features of subsequent conversation does suggest the difficulty of the ensuing small talk. It is at this point that Marya's consciousness opts out of the strain of it all, and focuses, rather, on the physical characteristics of someone totally unconnected with them:

> Marya gazed intently at a woman behind the counter and wondered whether she wore a wig or whether her hair had by some extraordinary freak of nature remained blonde, supple, and vital above her rather terrible mask of an avaricious and sensual old woman.

"If it's a wig," thought Marya, "it's the most marvellous one I've ever seen. It's darker at the roots. Can't be a wig." (p.108)

Such a detailed description suggests that this is more than a mere wandering of attention. It bears the signs of a moment of real abstraction in which Marya is, for a time, oblivious of what is going on around her. This ability to shift the focus of thought is a mental safety-valve – a moment of escape from the unwelcome tension which is building up around her. The digression develops a little before Marya, refreshed by it, can bear to return to the scene unfolding at her own table:

> She stared at the woman, who was arranging a huge green bow round the neck of a minute and hairy dog that stood on the counter, shivering violently. Then she listened again to the careful and nervous conversation of her three companions, and every time she heard Lois's sharply patronising accents a feeling of such intense irritation shot through her that she clenched her hands under the table.

Thus, the signs of tension in Marya also begin to manifest themselves physically, and so violent is the pressure of them that the only means of release now available to her is to make a fractious demand for a cognac. Stephan's response to her request elicits the disapproval of Heidler, and Lois's reaction characterises her affectation of disdain. This short exchange forms a perfect cameo in the text, brilliantly achieved in the narrative – a moment of almost open hostility which erupts between the embarrassed silences:

> "For God's sake," she said suddenly, "ask the waiter for a *fine*; I'm so thirsty."
> Stephan began to protest. "Don't have a brandy, Mado. She oughtn't to drink brandy, you know . . ." Heidler gave him a furious glance; Lois lifted her eyebrows.
> "*Garçon, une fine pour Madame.*"
> Another silence.

The 'silence' which follows put the seal on the evening, and again the narrator occupies this complete breakdown in communication with a digression. The perfect irony of the violinist's melody

encapsulates the bitterness of the message which the evening has
held:

> The violin wailed with pathos: 'Laugh, Pagliacci, for your love
> is ended.'
> Three girls passed the table, disappeared into a door marked
> telephone and emerged shortly afterwards, relieved, powdered
> and smiling, their lips very red. The woman behind the counter
> kissed her dog very passionately, calling it the *fille de sa mémère*.

The detail of 'the woman behind the counter' links the focalisation
here with that earlier instance, and thus the point of view may
again be identified as Marya's. The effect of the passage as a little
light relief after the traumatic scene narrowly avoided, is due not
only to the very commonplace nature of the observation about the
three girls, but also to the quasi-comic aspect of the woman's overt
fondness for her dog.

With Stephan's own assertiveness having been rendered ineffec-
tive by the Heidlers, it is up to them to wind the evening up, and
they dismiss him totally in the process. Lois makes the first move
to go, but she is relieved of the burden of closing out the scene by
her husband's dominance:

> Lois looked round her in an undecided fashion, fixed her eyes
> on a wall painting and murmured: "Well, I'm afraid . . ."
> "You're coming back with us, aren't you?" said Heidler to
> Marya with authority. "We'll drop you at your hotel."
> She looked at Stephan. He made a quick movement: "You're
> very kind, Monsieur," he said; "I'll take her home."
> "Oh, I think she'd better come with us," answered Heidler,
> staring over Stephan's head. "It's all on the way."
> "And it's pouring with rain," added Lois.
> "I'll meet you at the little restaurant near the Panthéon
> tomorrow, Stephan," said Marya without looking at him.
> (pp.108–9)

The final blow is delivered to Stephan by the refusal of either
Heidler or Marya to look at him as they speak. Thus, his reduction
is complete when even his own wife, guided by her passion for
another man, ceases to have any regard for his personal feelings.
And so, with the text relentlessly omitting any reference to his

inner life, the picture of Stephan 'staring after them' in an attitude of powerless bewilderment, makes a very striking end to the section:

> The three got up. The violin was still wailing. Stephan bowed. Heidler muttered something, looking rather awkward. At the door, she looked back and saw her husband leaning forward staring after them. (p.109)

Marya's act of looking back does increase the sense of pathos about this rejection. It is a gesture of regret – of one whose emotions are in a turmoil – and thus it is not surprising when, a little later in the evening, she leaves the Heidlers to rejoin Stephan. But the violinist's tune, 'still wailing', strikes the death knell of her relationship with her husband, so that the very next time that we see them together he senses that her love for him is 'ended'.

The real significance of the refrain 'Laugh, Pagliacci, for your love is ended', is not limited to Marya's love for Stephan, however. In the débâcle to follow its haunting lyricism which seems to point to some universal meaning, Heidler, during their very next meeting, informs Marya of the end of their affair. Again Marya's efforts to distance herself from the uncomfortable truth may be seen in operation here, so that the whole incident is played down as much as possible, although by that very effort, the pain of the separation seems to be magnified. As a whole, the passage presents a study in suffering, the effectiveness of which is maintained throughout by a tight narrative control of the emotion.

The choice of a café, a public place, in which to bring the affair to an end, is a particularly cruel stroke on the part of Heidler. For narrative purposes, however, it makes for increased tension, and thus it has greater dramatic potential. Marya will have to bear the pressure of public scrutiny on her, and this may act as a curb to her emotions, or alternatively, the burden of it, coupled with that of the distressing news, could prove to be too great for her to endure it with equanimity. Heidler, however, knows her well and takes the risk.

The first point which he establishes is that Stephen has departed for Amsterdam. This is his second significantly cruel stroke. As the scene unfolds, he will make it clear to Marya that not only is his affair with her at an end, but also that he does not want her to have anything more to do with her husband. Far from encouraging

Marya to join Stephan in Holland, a possible solution to the problem, instead he makes provision to send her in the opposite direction, to the South of France, 'to forget everything and get well'. The narrator prepares us for the bad news by creating an atmosphere of condolence in the surroundings: 'A waiter with a benevolent eye brought the coffee and brandies. From the farther side of the café, where Jimmie's Jazz performed nightly, the sound of music reached them faintly, and as it were with regret.' Thus, again, a background of music which is reminiscent of 'Laugh, Pagliacci, for your love is ended', accompanies the action as it unfolds. Marya, sensing the worst, attempts to bring Heidler to the point, and, taking this opportunity, he breaks the news to her. But his words are not directly rendered in the text:

> "Are you vexed with me?" asked Marya.
> "Not at all," answered Heidler. He cleared his throat. "My dear Mado ..." He began to talk dispassionately and with a certain relief, as though he were saying something which he had often longed to say. Towards the end of his explanation he became definite, even brutal, though not to excess. All the time that he was speaking she was looking into his eyes. (p.114)

This reduction of Heidler's words goes even further than a transposition into narratised speech; indeed, his utterance is completely obliterated from the text, so that all the reader is left with is an indication of the manner in which he speaks. And yet, the overall impression which is created is not one of an important omission. So inevitable must his words have been that we do not feel that we have missed anything by not having heard them for ourselves. The actual reduction places Heidler on the same narrative level as Stephan. This implies that he is becoming a generic male in Marya's mind – that he is making the speech which they all make when they dismiss a woman from their lives, and that there is no point in the narrative reproducing this speech since its contents are predictable.

Unlike her earlier inability to look at Stephan while arranging to meet him on the day following their rendezvous with the Heidlers, here Marya acts with a composure which brings a certain edge to her words: 'All the time that he was speaking she was looking into his eyes. Then she said slowly: "You're horribly treacherous, Heidler. I suppose you can't help it. I don't suppose you even know it. But you are."' By comparison with her relative equanimity, his own response in the face of such criticism reveals the immaturity and petulance of his character:

> "I'm not being treacherous; I'm being cruel perhaps," he added, not without complacency. "But I'm, not being treacherous. I've never shared a woman in my life, not knowingly anyhow, and I'm not going to start now."
> He folded his arms over his chest and looked across into one of the mirrors.
> "You forced me to share you," said Marya, "for months. Openly and ridiculously. You used your wife to torture me with."
> He answered coldly: "I don't know what you mean." And she saw that it was true.
> Then she said: "But H.J., I – I love you."
> "You haven't behaved as though you did," answered Heidler. "And it's too late now." He began to talk again – more emphatically, as if her persistence irritated him.
> "How cold it is in here," said Marya when he stopped. (p.115)

Throughout this exchange, Heidler's selfishness is exposed in his utterances. His refusal to see anyone's point of view but his own, and his arrogant dismissal of Marya's declaration of love for him, are both self-inflicted wounds which damage his integrity in our eyes. Marya's recognition of his obtuseness demonstrates her own resignation to it, and the implication of a further omission of his words from the text is that it is useless to argue with one who suffers from a congenital deficiency. The wonderful irrelevance of her concluding comment above, speaks volumes.

Now we are given an insight into Marya's thoughts as Heidler rambles on, mutely as far as the narrative is concerned. Again, unhappy with what is going on at her particular table, she has disengaged herself from it:

> The odd thing was that sitting on a café bench opposite was a little man whom she had met when she first came to Paris five years before, a little, yellow, wizened man and his name was – she couldn't remember – something like Monferrat, Monlisson, Mon . . . something.

The clear shift in narrative level here, to that of free indirect style, marks the absolute divorce of her consciousness from attention to Heidler's monologue. The obsessiveness with which she tries to remember the name is a further sign of the level of her abstraction at this point: 'It seemed to her enormously important that she should remember the name of the little man who, staring at her, was obviously also thinking: "Who is she, where have I met her?"' That she should stress the importance of this effort to remember his name, a matter of irrelevance, is an indication of her struggle to keep herself from thinking about the implications of Heidler's words. Gradually, however, the physical discomfort brought on by the shock – the tears which cloud her sight of the 'little man', and the 'cold' which she feels – impinge upon her consciousness, and she is forced to conclude her digression by remembering the name and returning to Heidler:

> She couldn't see his face clearly. There was a mist round it. Her hands were so cold that she felt them through the thin stuff of her dress. Mon. Monvoisin, that was it.
> Heidler was saying in a low voice: "I have a horror of you. When I think of you I feel sick."

Some compensation for having to make this necessary return may be gleaned from the ironic effect which the bathos of his words achieves at this point in the narrative. Again, the very ludicrousness of Heidler helps her to distance herself from him:

> He was large, invulnerable, perfectly respectable. Funny to think that she had lain in his arms and shut her eyes because she dared no longer look into his so terribly and wonderfully close. She began to laugh. After all, what did you do when the man you loved said a thing like that? You laughed, obviously.

So, the full significance of the violinist's refrain begins to be felt – 'Laugh, Pagliacci, for your love is ended.' And thus the laughter may be seen not only as a means of release from the tension felt by Marya, but also as a sardonic comment on the ephemerality of love, when its meaning, therefore, becomes more universal. Now Marya can abstract a ritual significance from the setting chosen by Heidler:

She said, still laughing: "So this is the *café fine* of rupture."

"It is," said Heidler; "don't get hysterical about it."

"Why hysterical?" asked Marya. "I can laugh if I want to, I suppose. You're funny enough to make anybody laugh sometimes."

"Of course, laugh. Laugh, but don't cry at the same time."

"Oh, am I crying?" she said, surprised. She put her hand up to her face. (p.116)

But Marya's efforts to distance herself are undermined by her emotions, and the realisation that she is again in danger of breaking down stimulates another escape, this time into memory:

Monsieur Monovoisin was gazing at her with an expression of avid curiosity. She began to remember all about Monsieur Monvoisin. He was one of Stephan's friends. They had been out together one night, the four of them; Monsieur Monvoisin had brought a girl called Lisette and they had wandered from bar to bar till four o'clock in the morning. A very tall young man had joined the party, who had hummed *"Si j'étais roi"* all the time. The jingling tune began to run in her head.

The repetition of 'Monsieur Monvoisin' three times in fairly rapid succession, acts as a focal device which helps Marya to fix her attention onto the digression. The memory elicited is a natural concomitant of the sense of rejection which she feels – shut out by her current lover, she remembers the calm of her life with his predecessor. But the level of abstraction which she achieves is not enough to enable her to redirect her thoughts for very long, although it does help her to adopt an ironic and careless attitude:

"Awfully funny," she remarked to Heidler; "do you see that man opposite? Well, I know him and he knows me. And he knows, I'm sure, that you are *plaquéing* me. And so does the waiter. Isn't *plaquer* a good word?"

"Very," he said. "Now pull yourself together, because we've got several things to talk about." He looked away from her and added uncomfortably: "You haven't got to worry, you know."

"What?" said Marya. "Oh, yes. Well, you can write to me about that. Let's go now, shall we?"

In Marya's cool reaction to the subject of money, something of the depth of her distress may be appreciated. Throughout the novel, her concern over her lack of finances has been genuine and deeply felt. Consequently, her seeming indifference to the question now, appears to be out of character, and must be taken to be a measure of the pain beside which all other worries pale into insignificance. Heidler too, who knows her well, is surprised by her reaction; indeed, he finds it quite unnerving:

> He seemed surprised and taken aback and made a feeble detaining gesture.
> "Wait a minute, wait a minute."
> She turned and looked at him, and when he saw her eyes he put his hand up to his tie, fidgeted with it and said: "Oh God! Oh God!"
> She passed her tongue over her dry lips, put her handkerchief into her bag and shut it carefully.

From this point until the end of the scene, Marya retains her composure and the upper hand, in contrast to the dithering Heidler who only manages to make a gesture of control when they are at last outside the café:

> He began talking again, hurriedly and uncertainly.
> "Look here, Marya, don't suppose . . . I want you to go down South to get well, to forget everything and get well. It's the only thing, believe me. Will you?"
> "No," said Marya.
> "Well, I beg you to."
> "No."
> "Why not?"
> "I'm very tired," Marya said, "I want to go."
> Outside the café he told her: "Get your things packed," then he turned and left her. (pp.116–17)

Needless to say, making an exit is all that is left to him to do in the face of such recalcitrance. But Marya's attitude is not born of a wish to be as difficult as possible; it is, as we have seen, a reaction against the pain she feels, and this section clearly shows her steady withdrawal into herself. The fatigue which she experiences at the end of it is a sign of the ensuing inertia which characterises the passivity to come from a sense of despair. This allows her to be despatched to Cannes by Heidler, despite her protestations, and it also accounts for her subsequent return to Paris when, for the moment, Stephan adopts an active role and arranges the journey.

By the time she returns, however, Marya's sense of torpor has taken a real hold on her, so that, far from making good her relationship with Stephan, she feels powerless to perform even the slightest action. The depths to which her passivity leads her are clearly seen in her failure to leave the café after a conversation with Monsieur Bernadet, her husband's friend. Instead of leaving when he leaves, she sits for a while, bewildered and 'tired'. In this passage, immediately prior to the final dramatic scene between Marya and Stephan, Heidler makes his last appearance in the text, although his presence is at its most indirect and reduced:

> After a time she took Heidler's letter out of her bag and looked at it. He had written: "I'm sending this to the Hôtel du Bosphore and hope you'll get it. I'm worried about you. Why have you come back to Paris so suddenly? Will you let me know where and when we can meet? I am only too anxious to do all I can to help you. Please believe that." (pp.136–7)

Here, rather than the entire letter being reproduced in the text, a feature which has so far been observed regarding all of Heidler's letters to Marya, its content is cut in accordance with the section which she chooses to read. Thus, the narrative level is altered, and his words are placed at a further remove than usual. This shift is indicated textually through the use of quotation marks. What the reader actually receives is a quotation from the letter as it filters through Marya's consciousness. Subsequently, in contrast to this distance achieved between Heidler's thoughts and their presentation in the text, a further shift into free indirect style makes for a more immediate rendering of Marya's thought processes:

> When and where? In some café, of course. The unvarying background. Knowing waiters, clouds of smoke, the smell of drink. She would sit there trembling, and he would be cool, a little impatient, perhaps a little nervous. Then she would try to explain and he would listen with a calm expression. Top dog. (p.137)

In this, the conditional tense indicates another alteration in narrative level – a prolepsis[9] which, in the course of the narrative, will turn out to be frustrated, owing to the fact that Marya will not actually meet Heidler again. In the text, however, this shift may be seen to account for an instance of Heidler's presence at its most indirect:

> "Of course you want money" he would be thinking. "Naturally. How much? I'm willing to give the traditional sum, the sum which is right and proper under the circumstances, and no more. Well, talk. I'm listening"

But the sustainment of this prolepsis points towards Marya's own complex level of abstraction. She is no longer distracted by observable detail, such as the three girls going to the powder-room, or even by the memory of an incident which had actually occurred in her life; but she now allows herself to become absorbed by a daydream, an anticipation which, as it turns out, will never be realised. On the one hand, this points to an even deeper withdrawal from reality, given that the subject of her reverie is now created out of the fabric of her own imagination. On the other hand, however, it does show Marya's ironic awareness of the position of women in society, and it is thus concerned with a more general reality. She is able to relate her own particular position to what is the 'traditional' expectation of men and women in patriarchy. And it is this irony which is the means by which Rhys suggests the oppressiveness of Marya's social position. Marya is passive in the sense in which society expects her, as a woman, to be passive. In the course of the novel, she is manipulated by two men – firstly, by Stephan, and then, when he is jailed, by Heidler. When the latter exerts his financial power over her, she is faced with no choice but to comply with his wishes. However, the capacity of her narrative eye to temper the portrait of Heidler with a degree of ironic humour identifies her attitude as a feminist one:

> She'd talk and all the time her eyes would be saying, "I loved you. I loved you. D'you remember?"
> But he wouldn't look at her eyes, or if he did he'd look away again very quickly. He'd be feeling healthy-minded, outrageously so. He'd long for cold baths and fresh air. Can't she explain and get it over?
> "Didn't I tell her that she made me feel sick? The extraordinary persistence of this type of woman."

Here, with the free indirect style of 'Can't she explain and get it over?', the narrator's imitation of Marya imitating Heidler takes the indirection with which Heidler is presented to an extreme.

In *Quartet*, the moments of such overt relation to a more general social reality are few. It is possible to read the novel and to feel that Marya was merely unlucky in her experiences with men, and that if she had met different people, things would have worked out better for her. I should now like to turn to *After Leaving Mr Mackenzie*, a novel in which the main character is more contextualised than Marya was. We see Julia Martin in the context of her family and, where Mackenzie is concerned, in relation to patriarchy. A feeling that there is nothing very special about Mackenzie, or indeed about the circumstances of his relationship with Julia, underlines our increasing awareness that this particular Rhys woman is an underdog confronting the whole social system.

3
Julia and the 'Others'

In *After Leaving Mr Mackenzie* the portrait of Julia Martin is developed with a good deal more ambiguity than that of Marya in *Quartet*. Although in many parts of the text there is an identification of her consciousness with the narrative voice, this is balanced by the fact that in other parts she is focused on externally through the eyes of minor characters who are themselves rendered with a greater degree of complexity than was the case in the earlier novel. Thus, where Julia is concerned, there is a greater resistence to being read than there was with Marya, and consequently the reader does not always know quite what to make of her.

I should like to begin my analysis of this novel by focusing briefly on Julia's awareness of herself as an underdog confronting the whole social system before I go on to reinforce this idea by examining in detail her relationships with two representatives of that system. In Mackenzie's dealings with her we will see her relating to patriarchy, while her sister, Norah, will show her in the context of her family. These two alternative views of Julia add a significant dimension to her portrait. However, they are not without their own narrative reduction, and therefore they do not simplify our response to her, but rather add to our increasing sense that judgement of character is an uncertain affair.

The difficulty of reading Julia is hinted at early in the text in a comment on the position of the window in her bed-sit:

> Julia paid sixteen francs a night. Her room on the second floor was large and high-ceilinged, but it had a sombre and one-eyed aspect because the solitary window was very much to one side. (p.7)

The application of human characteristics in the description of this window suggests an indirect authorial comment on Julia's recognition that the world in which she lives is askew. The implication is that her point of view, represented by the restricted outlook, is somehow limited, and that consequently her view of things will be distorted, but that this is a perspective which has been developed by an engagement with such a perverse world, that is, by one who is fully immersed in the system. This is an important departure from the almost wholly sympathetic attitude of the narrator to Marya in *Quartet*, and it does point towards a more critical treatment both of the heroine and, indeed, of the social system itself in this later novel.

More criticism of the system, both implicit and overt, emerges in a short passage which accounts for the ritual of 'Tuesday morning at half-past nine' when 'Liliane, the chamber-maid would bring up the letter from Mr Mackenzie's solicitor on a tray with coffee and a croissant.' The irony of the position of the cheque – next to the sustenance which it buys – is only fully appreciated on a second reading when the contents of the letter are known. Similarly, the gravity of a definite article which bestows an added sense of importance upon '*the* letter' (my italics) is ironic in tone. This importance, however, is undercut when the development of the section moves on to concern itself with a description of the chambermaid rather than with the communication in the envelope:

> She was a big, fair girl, sullen and rather malicious because she worked without stopping from six in the morning until eleven or twelve at night, and because she knew that, being plain, she would probably have to work like that until she died. (p.10)

This omniscient insight is well placed. In juxtaposition between the delivery and the revelation of the contents of the letter, it implicitly points to the unfairness of a system which allows discrimination to operate in favour of those women who happen to be physically attractive to men. It is not surprising, therefore, that the 'plain' Liliane should show her resentment at having to wait on Julia, by 'banging the door' on her exit.

But the social oppression of women is not quite as clear-cut as Liliane would have us believe. Julia, who is not 'plain', and who is therefore able to make use of her sexual attractiveness to get a better life for herself, is no less subjected to oppression than the wretched chambermaid. When we see her in relation to Mackenzie, this becomes abundantly clear. We notice it first in her response to his letters, and it is here that we are given a physical description of her:

As she read a strained, anxious expression never left her face, which was round and pale with deep, bluish circles under the eyes. Her eyebrows were thin, finely marked; her very thick dark hair was lit by too red highlights and stood out rather wildly round her head. Her hands were slender, narrow-palmed with very long fingers, like the hands of an oriental. (pp.10–11)

Unlike Marya, whose 'blonde' and 'full-lipped' face suggests the stereotype of the English rose, the circles under Julia's eyes, and the vivid henna highlights, present a less romantic notion of the heroine. Apart from the lines of strain, we are told that her physical features are so unrevealing that any attempt to classify her in terms of 'age', 'nationality', or 'social background' is doomed to failure. This, of course, makes for a definite resistance to being read. And the painstaking way in which she applies her make-up is not, itself, without a significance symbolic of her withdrawal from scrutiny:

She made herself up elaborately and carefully; yet it was clear that what she was doing had long ceased to be a labour of love and had become partly a mechanical process, partly a substitute for the mask she would have liked to wear. (p.11)

Just as Julia's room represents 'a good sort of place to hide in', so too the ritual of the daily application of the make-up becomes the donning of a shield to act as a barrier between her real self and the external world. Wearing this 'mask' enables her to present a persona to the world and engage in it while at the same time protecting her own sense of identity by covering it up. The physical withdrawal, however, is incomplete, for no matter how much 'kohl' she applies to her eyes, it cannot conceal the expression in them:

Her eyes gave her away. By her eyes and the deep circles under them you saw that she was a dreamer, that she was vulnerable – too vulnerable ever to make a success of a career of chance.

By contrast, the eyes of the 'woman on the floor above', whom Julia fears herself coming to resemble should she let herself go, are 'malevolent – the horribly malevolent eyes of an old, forsaken woman.' Like Liliane, this woman presents another contrast to

Julia. Unlike the waitress, however, she has a 'humble, cringing manner' which is born of a lack of both 'money' and 'virtue'. Perhaps, in years to come, Liliane's arrogance will temper itself into this sort of self-abasement, although the implication is that whereas Liliane's attitude is born of the despair of ever getting out of the social rut in which she finds herself, this woman's mood comes from the bitterness of having been rejected in love: 'She was a shadow, kept alive by a flame of hatred for somebody who had long ago forgotten all about her.' Herein lies the lesson for Julia. And here, too, is the beginning of a theme which will grow as the novel develops. This 'shadow', of whom Julia is constantly aware, will gradually evolve into an image having a skeletal form, and such ideas of death will haunt her.

Julia's awareness of the system is not without its own irony. It is her financial dependence upon Mackenzie which frightens her most about her social position. When he gives notice that he intends to withdraw his support, both her fear and her irony are demonstrated in a revealing image of imprisonment:

> She had always expected that one day they would do some-
> thing like this. Yet, now that it had happened, she felt bewil-
> dered, as a prisoner might feel who has resigned himself to
> solitary confinement for an indefinite period in a not uncomfort-
> able cell and who is told one morning, "Now, then, you're going
> to be let off today. Here's a little money for you. Clear out."
> (p.14)

Thus, she feels stifled by her dependence upon Mackenzie, and yet completely lost without it. Her fear should not be underestimated. Its physical effect is shown when she actually makes an effort to confront him. Her awareness of Mackenzie and his lawyer working as a team against her is an awareness of patriarchy at its most sinister and oppressive:

> At the sight of him Julia's heart began to beat furiously and her
> legs trembled. She was excited to an almost unbearable degree,
> for, added to her other emotions, was the fact that she was very
> much afraid both of him and of his lawyer. When she thought of
> the combination of Mr Mackenzie and Maître Legros, all sense of
> reality deserted her and it seemed to her that there were no
> limits at all to their joint powers of defeating and hurting her.

Together, the two perfectly represented organized society, in which she had no place and against which she had not a dog's chance. (p.17)

Such an overt awareness of her own oppressed position is made possible in a passage in which the perspective is her own. On Mackenzie's emergence into the text, however, the narrative resumes its external point of view for a while, until it makes inroads into his consciousness. This shift allows a tone of comic irony to colour with a little light relief what is, for Julia, a very painful meeting.

Mr Mackenzie was a man of medium height and colouring. He was of the type which proprietors of restaurants and waiters respect. He had enough nose to look important, enough stomach to look benevolent. His tips were not always in proportion with the benevolence of his stomach, but this mattered less than one might think.

In such a humorous fashion we discover that 'Mr Mackenzie was comfortably off, but no millionaire', that he had retired early after having been set up in business by his father, and that he had moved to Paris despite his feelings of xenophobia for the French. All in all, the portrait of Mackenzie is one of an independent, self-satisfied bon viveur, whose pretentiousness throughout is punctured by the ironic wit of the narrator:

... Mr Mackenzie answered with a smile that he had trained not to be bashful ... (p.17)

... He was not one of those people who regard the making of money as an adventure and cannot stop and do something else. He had made a fair sufficiency and then retired. (p.18)

... he had adopted a certain mental attitude, a certain code of morals and manners, from which he seldom departed. He did depart from it, but only when he was practically certain that nobody would know that he had done so.

His code was perfectly adapted to the social system and in any argument he could have defended it against any attack whatsoever. However, he never argued about it, because that was part of the code.

Mr Mackenzie's code, philosophy or habit of mind would have been a complete protection to him had it not been for some kink in his nature – that volume of youthful poems perhaps still influencing him – which morbidly attracted him to strangeness, to recklessness, even unhappiness. (pp.18–19)

Already we notice a difference in approach here from that adopted by the narrator in *Quartet* where Hugh Heidler, who occupies a similar diegetic position to Mackenzie, was treated with a good deal less humorous irony. A consequence of this is that despite the gloomy nature of the content in *After Leaving Mr Mackenzie*, the subtlety of the writing makes it a more amusing novel to read than *Quartet*. The complexity of the art allows for a much more serious engagement with each of the main characters than was possible in the first work. Here, for example, Mackenzie emerges as a man full of faults, but a shift in focus to his own point of view throws light onto his motivation and character, fleshing out his persona into a more fully rounded whole than was the case with Heidler. Furthermore, the shift, which takes effect from section 5 onwards, allows for an alternative view of Julia. This, in itself, is a development from the first novel where Marya was hardly ever seen through other eyes. In *After Leaving Mr Mackenzie* the alternative viewpoint is sustained, and the approach becomes a feature of the novel when the opinions of other characters, too, are rendered in order to balance those of Julia.

The alteration of narrative level into Mackenzie's consciousness brings the reader certain background detail about his former relationship with Julia. His thoughts on the subject are triggered off by the location – 'the last time he had seen her had been in that restaurant' – and thus an increased potential for dramatic irony is anticipated, for the reader knows, as Mackenzie himself does not, that she is about to confront him again.

The occasional movement into free indirect style sets up an immediate relationship between the narrator and the character, allowing the reader direct access to Mackenzie's thoughts; but these moments are always tempered by a subsequent narrative irony which checks our sympathy, keeping the reader constantly aware of the moral blindness of Mackenzie's motives:

An insanity! Looking back on it he thought, "My God, why did I do it? Why did I want to sleep with her?" Yet there was no getting away from it; for a time she had obsessed him. He had lied; he had made her promises which he never intended to keep; and so on, and so on. All part of the insanity, for which he was not responsible. (p.19)

And again:

> Yet she wasn't the hard-bitten sort. She was the soft sort. Anyone could tell that. Afraid of life. Had to screw herself up to it all the time. He had liked that at first. Then it had become a bit of a bore.

The shift in point of view allows the narrative to present certain details of Julia's background incidentally rather than in a formal narratisation as was the case in *Quartet*. Thus, the reader learns this information because Mackenzie chooses to recollect it in his reflections on the past:

> Julia had told him that she had married and had left England immediately after the armistice. She had had a child. The child had died – in Central Europe, somewhere – and then she had separated from her husband and had divorced him or been divorced by him, Mr Mackenzie could not gather which. Or perhaps she had never really been married at all. In any case she had come to Paris alone. (pp.19–20)

Here, the movement noted above, where the effects of free indirect style precede and are punctured by narrative irony, is in inverse order. In this case, Mr Mackenzie's thoughts are initially reduced into transposed speech in indirect style, before being liberated from the bonds of narratisation. The ironic effect of 'Mr Mackenzie could not gather which', however, colours the subsequent 'free' utterance, giving it an unmistakably bitchy tone. Oddly enough, throughout the novel, even in moments where the point of view is his own, Mackenzie is never referred to by his Christian name. This has a comic effect. The absurd implication of the free indirect style being that Mackenzie is the sort of person who probably thinks of himself as 'Mr Mackenzie', it underlines his pomposity. However, it also preserves a distance between him and the narrator, which is peculiar to their relationship. By contrast, although similar social niceties are observed in the case of Mr

Horsfield, we are at least told very early on that his Christian name is George;[1] furthermore, despite his similar diegetic position to that of Mackenzie, Julia herself addresses W. Neil James Esq. as 'My dear Neil' on the occasion of her writing to him.[2]

As the section draws to a close, the potential for dramatic irony is intensified, firstly through Mackenzie's memory of the 'scene' which Julia had created in that particular restaurant when he had broken his relationship with her:

> Julia had wept; she had become hysterical. She had made a scene, sitting in that very restaurant, under the shocked and disapproving eyes of Monsieur Albert. She had made him look a fool. (p.21)

The intensity of his own sense of humiliation is compounded by the recollection that he had sent her some indiscreet and excessively emotional letters, and the depth of his feeling of embarrassment is reflected textually, again through free indirect style:

> A feeling of caution and suspicion which almost amounted to hatred had entirely overcome him. He had definitely suspected her of hoarding some rather foolish letters which he had written and which she had insisted that she had torn up. One of the letters had begun, 'I would like to put my throat under your feet.' He wriggled when he thought of it. Insanity! Forget it; forget it.

Such a direct quotation from one of the letters, thus taken out of context, serves two purposes: by the very lurid banality of its cliché it punctures Mackenzie's pretentiousness, his 'superior' attitude; it also gives an insight into the wholly sexual nature of his earlier obsession with Julia. Having said that, however, the detail of his response on recalling his indiscretion, brilliantly captured in the term 'wriggled', is of universal significance; undoubtedly, readers will respond sympathetically to Mackenzie on recognising similar feelings of humiliation in their own past. Certainly, this passage has been written by one who knows what it is to squirm with embarrassment.

Nevertheless, the narrative irony is relentless, and immediately following this detail of Mackenzie's excess is the barbed observation that 'Caution was native to him'. Despite any sympathy for

him which may be evoked, the reader is not allowed to forget
Mackenzie's guilt:

> She haunted him, as an ungenerous action does haunt one,
> though Mr Mackenzie persisted in telling himself that he had not
> been ungenerous. Ungenerous! That was all nonsense. (pp.21–2)

In this observation, the theme of death is now connected to Julia
herself, who, in Mackenzie's perception, becomes the spectre. This
imaginatively foreshadows the development of the idea of mortal-
ity which began with Julia's awareness of others as the 'shadow'.
Gradually, as the novel develops, Julia will lose her own sense of
identity and become one of the living dead, existing in barren
isolation where genuine relationships with other people are not
possible. For the moment, however, she retains enough of a sense
of purpose to haunt Mackenzie physically by engaging in a direct
confrontation with him; and the section ends dramatically with her
appearance in the restaurant: 'Then he lifted his eyes from the veal
– and there she was, coming in at the door.' This conclusion has
something of the same hermeneutic sense of suspense which
informs many of the section endings in *Quartet*. Generally, however, the action in *After Leaving Mr Mackenzie* is not propelled in this
way, and consequently its use on this occasion is all the more
noticeable. The effect is parodic, not only of a particular type of
melodrama, but also, we may feel, of the writer's own earlier style.

The anticipated confrontation occurs in section 6, when with
superb artistic control, Jean Rhys renders the scene with an
exquisite irony which is both comic and painful in effect. The
unique quality of the passage is made possible only by the
narrative shift into Mackenzie's consciousness, for, had the point
of view remained with Julia, the peculiar internal tensions established in the previous section would have been missing, and the
effect of the whole would have suffered considerably.

The association of death with Julia in Mackenzie's mind is
developed here in his perception of her as she enters the restaurant:

> She walked in – pale as a ghost. She went straight up to Mr
> Mackenzie's table, and sat down opposite to him. He opened his
> mouth to speak, but no words came. So he shut it again. He was
> thinking, "Oh God, oh Lord, she's come here to make a

scene. . . . Oh God, oh Lord, she's come here to make a scene."
(p.22)

Julia, seen thus externally throughout the section, is made to
resemble something of a spectre whose movements are observed
but whose motivation remains a mystery. This has a dislocating
effect, for the reader is used to a narrative orientation from her
point of view in the scenes in which she is present. Such a
disturbance, then, adds to the unusual effect of the entire passage.
With the domination of the supernatural, it is Julia who is seen to
retain the upper hand, leaving Mackenzie himself in an attitude of
astonished impotence, opening and closing his mouth indecisive-
ly, little knowing how best to take control. The narrative repetition
of his thoughts demonstrates the turmoil of his mind, which is
further reflected in the anxiety of his behaviour:

> He looked to the right and the left of him with a helpless
> expression. He felt a sensation of great relief when he saw that
> Monsieur Albert was standing near his table and looking at him
> with significance.

The initial feeling of relief on recognising an ally, however, is soon
dissipated on the recollection of his earlier humiliation which had
been witnessed by this man, and as a reaction, his usual attitude of
superiority reasserts itself:

> "That's the first time I've ever seen that chap look straight at
> anybody," Mr Mackenzie thought.
> Monsieur Albert was a small, fair man, an Alsatian. His eyes
> telegraphed, "I understand; I remember this woman. Do you
> want to have her put out?"
> Mr Mackenzie's face instinctively assumed a haughty expres-
> sion, as if to say, "What the devil do you mean?" He raised his
> eyebrows a little, just to put the fellow in his place.

The brief narrative departure into detail of Albert's physical stature
is not insignificant. No doubt, added to Mackenzie's sense of
discomfort on recalling that his earlier embarrassment had been
observed is a snobbish horror of needing help from one of the
lower orders. Subsequent to the implied reprimand in his de-
meanour, however, is a comic anticlimax when he realises that he
may need assistance after all:

Monsieur Albert moved away. When he had gone a little distance, he turned. This time Mr Mackenzie tried to telegraph back, "Not yet, anyhow. But stand by."

When, at last, Mackenzie manages to look at Julia, it is she who maintains the upper hand by breaking the silence:

Then he looked at Julia for the first time. She said, "Well, you didn't expect to see me here, did you?"
She coughed and cleared her throat.
Mr Mackenzie's nervousness left him. When she had walked in silent and ghost-like, he had been really afraid of her. Now he only felt that he disliked her intensely. He said in rather a high-pitched voice, "I'd forgotten that I had invited you, certainly. However, as you are here, won't you have something to eat?"

The physical volume of her voice, together with her flesh and blood cough, reassures Mackenzie who is now able to retaliate with a certain sarcasm. However, the effect of his remark is undercut by the 'high-pitched' tenor of his voice. This emasculation lends further weight to the dominance of Julia's own position. Coolly, she refuses his invitation, but takes the opportunity to help herself to his wine. The gesture is quite arrogant in its casualness:

Julia shook her head.
There was a second place laid on the table. She took up the carafe of wine and poured out a glass. Mr Mackenzie watched her with a sardonic expression. He wondered why the first sight of her had frightened him so much. He was now sure that she could not make much of a scene. He knew her; the effort of walking into the restaurant and seating herself at his table would have left her in a state of collapse. (p.23)

Mackenzie's 'sardonic' posture, affected in an effort to cover up his initial discomfiture, is misplaced. His assessment of Julia's motive for coming into the restaurant is inaccurate, she has not come to cause a 'scene'; and as the passage develops, his own weakness of character will be demonstrated, in contrast to Julia's relative strength. Already, his attitude of contempt begins to lessen as a subconscious sense of guilt manifests itself in his inclination to 'justify himself':

"But why do it?" thought Mr Mackenzie. "Why in the name of common sense do a thing like that?"

Then he felt a sudden wish to justify himself, to let her know that he had not been lying when he had told her that he was going away.

He said, "I only got back a couple of weeks ago."

But Julia's response shows an utter disdain for him. By completely ignoring his comment and changing the subject, she manages to unsettle him totally:

Julia said, "Tell me, do you really like life? Do you think it's fair? Honestly now, do you?"

He did not answer this question. What a question, anyway! He took up his knife and fork and began to eat. He wanted to establish a sane and normal atmosphere.

This momentary shift into free indirect style with 'What a question, anyway!" is tempered by an immediate return to the narratisation of Mackenzie's actions and motives. As the scene develops, a more frequent use of this narrative mode will be directed towards establishing a comic effect through the counterpointing of Julia's summary of her treatment at the hands of Legros, with a direct rendering of Mackenzie's thoughts on the subject. For the moment, however, the use of free indirect style is kept to a minimum.

The effect of Julia's question on Mackenzie's thought processes is seen in the simultaneity of two different ideas going through his mind. The linear contiguity of the narrative demands that for the sake of clarity these be rendered in succession in the text, but the point is made clearly that in the diegesis their actual occurrence is coexistent:

As he put small pieces of veal and vegetable into his mouth, he was telling himself that he might just let her talk on, finish his meal, pay the bill, and walk out. Or he might accompany her out of the restaurant at once, under pretext of finding a quieter place to discuss things. Or he might hint that if she did not go he would ask Monsieur Albert to put her out. Though, of course, it was rather late to do that now.

At the same time he was thinking, "No. Of course life isn't fair.

It's damned unfair, really. Everybody knows that, but what does she expect me to do about it? I'm not God Almighty."

The formality of this narrative arrangement is an indication of the writer's restrained use of free indirect style where Mackenzie is concerned. The liberating effect of it could have resulted in a textual rendering much closer to the actual diegetic simultaneity. However, the adopted mode here keeps Mackenzie's position in an ironic perspective which might have been lessened had we been given a more direct access to his thoughts. The narrative attention to detail which takes the trouble to indicate his external action while these complex thought processes are in operation paints a comic picture of him. There is something quite ludicrous in the 'small pieces of veal and vegetable' and the stasis which is achieved by the action merely of 'putting them into his mouth', not eating, chewing, or even swallowing them. Here, the suggestion of cannibalism which had been evoked in *Quartet* with Lois's assertion that 'eating is the greatest pleasure in life' (p.12), takes on a different tone. The narrative close-up of the actual feeding process robs it of any ritual glamour which the Heidlers may have wished to bestow upon it, and it is foregrounded in a particularly revolting fashion. The significance of the earlier parodic equation of Julia with the veal, which had brought the previous scene to a close, is now appreciated more fully. And following this comes another authorial comment upon Rhys's own earlier method, this time put in free indirect style into Mackenzie's words in response to Julia raising the subject of Legros:

She asked, "How's your pal, Maître Legros?"
"Very well indeed, I think," he said stiffly.
She began to talk volubly, in a low, rather monotonous voice. It was like a flood which has been long dammed up suddenly pouring forth.
He listened, half-smiling. Surely even she must see that she was trying to make a tragedy out of a situation that was fundamentally comical. The discarded mistress – the faithful lawyer defending the honour of the client.... A situation consecrated as comical by ten thousand farces and a thousand comedies. (pp.23–4)

The parody of melodrama, outlined here by Mackenzie, could

easily be converted to read: 'The discarded mistress – the faithful wife defending the honour of the husband . . .' and, as such, it would sum up part of the content of *Quartet*. Clearly, any fair assessment of the earlier novel may not reduce it to such a level, for there are many redeeming features,. as we saw in the previous chapter. In *After Leaving Mr Mackenzie* too, although, as Mackenzie himself points out, the content is still potentially melodramatic, distance is achieved to a certain extent by a play in the narrative, in which the very genre itself is parodied. Mackenzie's assertion that such content is comical is, of course, relative to one's own position; clearly, one would not expect 'the discarded mistress' to find it amusing, and he himself has found very little to laugh at in the evening so far. However, the comic aspect bestowed upon the experience by the ironic rendering of it does bring a whole new perspective to the situation, which the reader can appreciate while acknowledging the pain of it all. And this is what keeps that sense of melodrama in check.

Distance is also achieved when the situation is assessed by other characters than the main protagonist. Later, it will be the turn of George Horsfield, Norah, Miss Wyatt and Uncle Griffiths to give an opinion on Julia's life-style. In this section, however, judgement is left to Mackenzie:

> As far as he could make out she had a fixed idea that her affair with him and her encounter with Maître Legros had been the turning-point in her life. They had destroyed some necessary illusions about herself which had enabled her to live her curious existence with a certain amount of courage and audacity. (p.24)

Mackenzie's viewpoint which opens this paragraph is developed by what appears to be an authorial comment in the second sentence. Certainly, the latter assertion seems far too well informed to be his, and its positive disposition towards Julia seems quite out of keeping with his earlier scornful attitude. Over and above this, there seems to be a definite break in the narrative continuity between the end of this paragraph and the beginning of the next, which, on opening, remarks that Mackenzie is called back to attention:

> At the mention of Maître Legros Mr Mackenzie pricked up his ears, for he had only received three very business-like

communications from that gentleman, and he was rather curious
to know how French lawyers manage these affairs.

The ensuing monologue, therefore, in which Julia relates the tale of
her experience at the hands of Legros, is encouraged by Mackenzie
who sits silently throughout, until the very end, when he is
directly questioned. It is here that a narrative counterpoint is set up
in which Julia's statements are very much reduced into reported
speech while, through the devices of free indirect style and direct
speech, there is unimpeded access to Mackenzie's ironic thoughts.
This narrative arrangement has a humorous effect, and it is worth
quoting it in its entirety to retain the antiphonal quality of the
whole:

> She said that Maître Legros had bullied her about letters that
> she had destroyed and possible unpleasantness that she never
> intended to make.
> Well he probably had. For to put the fear of God into her was
> what he was paid for. On the other hand, if she had any sense
> she must have realized that three-quarters of it was bluff.
> She said that the lawyers had told the clerk to lock the door
> and send for an *agent*.
> He wondered whether to believe this, for he had a vague idea
> that locking doors is one of the things that is not legal.
> She said that he had threatened to have her deported, and had
> talked a great deal about the *police des moeurs*. She said that there
> had been a lot of clerks and typists in the room who had stared at
> her and laughed all the time.
> "A lot?" he thought. "Well, three or four at the outside."
> She said that she had begun to cry.
> Well in all careers one must be prepared to take the rough with
> the smooth.
> She said that she had been determined never to accept the
> money offered.
> "Well, well," thought Mr Mackenzie. *"Tiens, tiens."*
> She said that she had fallen ill, and then she hadn't cared
> about anything except to lie in peace and be ill. And then she had
> written to the lawyer and asked for the allowance to be sent to
> her. And after that something had gone *kaput* in her, and she
> would never be any good any more – never any more.

She raised her voice. "Why did you pay a lawyer to bully me?" she said.

Mr Mackenzie pushed away his plate. This was intolerable. He could not go on pretending to eat – not if she were going to say that sort of thing at the top of her voice. (pp.24–5)

The sheer entertainment value of this passage relies for its effect on the necessary reduction of Julia. Here, the distance between the actual event and its rendering in the narrative is great, and it operates on many levels. Firstly, unlike the technique in *Quartet*, where a potentially dramatic scene would have been rendered directly in the text, the confrontation between Julia and Legros, which occurs in the diegesis before the starting point of the first narrative, is subordinated in the text for six months of diegetic duration. Secondly, again unlike the approach in *Quartet*, where the device of a flashback would have compensated for any delay in the telling and thus allowed it to be rendered with immediacy, when it does appear in the narrative in *After Leaving Mr Mackenzie*, it is further subordinated into indirect speech. Thirdly, at this stage the narrative is orientated from the point of view of a character who was himself neither directly involved in the event, nor even well disposed towards the woman who recounts it. Furthermore, the potential for ambiguity is increased by the fact that this is the only time in the text when this incident is referred to. Mackenzie himself doubts the veracity of some of Julia's assertions, the locked door, for instance, and we also may wonder how much exaggeration there is in her account – did the clerks and typists really behave in that way, or did she, in a hypersensitive state, merely imagine it? But our own position is more complicated than Mackenzie's, for whereas he receives Julia's report at first hand, the version we obtain is mediated, firstly by his impression of it, and secondly by the narratisation of that view.

Remarkably, despite the comic effect achieved by the counterpointing, and the reduction of Julia's presence in the text, the view of her put forward here is not devoid of sympathy. Towards the end of her reported monologue, it is Mackenzie's turn to suffer subordination when his thoughts fall silent after the final ironic *'tiens'*. Indeed, in the last paragraph of her speech, there is a momentary alteration of narrative level into free indirect style, which brings us closer in touch with her own feelings. This occurs with the repetition of 'never, any more', which briefly suggests the bitterness of her emotions, and the pause in the utterance, indicated by the comma, dramatically adds to the sense of finality about the expression. But, the moment over, the regret is not dwelt upon, it is brought to an end with a sudden change in attitude which is signified by an increase in the volume of her voice and the utterance of a sardonic question. In this way, Julia maintains the upper hand, her triumph is made clear from the evident embarrassment of Mackenzie, whose gesture of pushing his plate away demonstrates his nervousness. Now there is a return to his point of view, and the comedy of the situation which, ironically in view of his earlier comments on the subject, remains hidden from Mackenzie, suggests itself to the reader. The real reason for his discomfort is shown to be his anticipated humiliation in front of people whom he knows:

> Besides, while she was talking, a chap whom he knew, a journalist called Moon, had come in with a friend, and was sitting two or three tables away. Moon was a gossip. He was talking volubly, and the friend, a thin, dark, youngish man, was glancing round the restaurant with rather a bored expression. At any moment the attention of these two might be attracted. Who knew to what wild lengths Julia would go? (p.25)

Thus, in this most indirect of ways, George Horsfield who, as it turns out, is the 'friend', is introduced into the text. The purpose of his introduction into this section will become evident in the next chapter when an alternative, and quite objective view of the confrontation between Julia and Mackenzie will be rendered. For the moment, however, his presence is subordinated to the more important development of the scene.

The free indirect style which brings the above paragraph to an end on a note of exaggeration, prepares for the extravagance of Mackenzie's private mental response, and makes the subsequent undercutting of it by the narrator's own sense of humour all the more comic:

> Mr Mackenzie thought, "Never again – never, never again – will I get mixed up with this sort of woman."
> His collar felt too tight for him. He thrust his chin out in an

instinctive effort to relieve the constriction. The movement was exactly like that of a horse shying.

From this point onwards, a tension is created through Mackenzie's neurotic fear of a 'scene', his suspicions about Julia's intentions, and the contrasting reality which is quite mild in actuality. At one stage, Mackenzie's stress, which the narrator foregrounds extravagantly in order to maintain a distance through comic irony, actually prevents him from taking the opportunity to play things down for the sake of appearances, which is offered to him by Julia's outstretched hand:

> He looked at Julia and a helpless, imploring expression came into his eyes. His hand was lying on the table. She put her hand on his, and said, in a very low voice, "You know, I've been pretty unhappy."
> At this change of attitude, Mr Mackenzie felt both relieved and annoyed. "She's trying to get hold of me again," he thought. "But what a way to do it! My God, what a way to do it!"
> He drew his hand away slowly, ostentatiously. Keeping his eyes fixed on hers, he deliberately assumed an expression of disgust. Then he cleared his throat and asked, "Well, what exactly did you want when you came in here?"

Mackenzie's biggest mistake here is to be so offensive in his rejection of Julia's gesture of reconciliation, for the opportunity will not come again. Instead, the affront which she feels is registered on her face, and from this moment, the former arrogance of her attitude – far cleverer in effect than his own scorn for her – reasserts itself:

> Julia grew paler. The hollows under her eyes were deeper. She looked much older. But Mr Mackenzie had no pity for her; she was a dangerous person. A person who would walk in and make an uncalled-for scene like this was a dangerous person. (pp.25–6)

Once more, Mackenzie misunderstands. Believing the alteration in her features to be an invitation to him to pity her, his response is to recoil, and again his reasoning betrays itself through its very extravagance. She, meanwhile, attempts to collect her thoughts; the effort of it is reflected in the hesitant manner of her speech:

> She said, "Oh, yes, look here, this cheque. . . . This cheque I
> got today. I don't want it."
> "Good," said Mr Mackenzie. "Just as you like, of course.
> You're the best judge of that."
> But he felt surprised and not at all pleased. He knew that
> hysteria ruled these people's lives, but he would never have
> thought that it would be carried to the extremity of giving up
> money. (p.26)

Here too, the calm of Mackenzie's agreement belies the activity of
his thoughts. Rejecting money is something foreign to his own
nature; we remember that he had gladly accepted financial help
from his father, and he cannot understand such reluctance in
others. This attitude in itself demonstrates the essential difference
of his orientation from that of Julia, and his arrogant acknowledgement of the divide is seen in his belittling reference to 'these
people'. Julia, however, has not finished. Having recovered from
the mistake of momentarily letting her defences down, she now
feels able to move towards the purpose of her meeting with him. In
full possession of her composure once more, she tortures Mackenzie, watching him squirm with frightened anticipation while she
prepares herself as leisurely as possible for what she has to say:

> "Wait a minute," she said. "That isn't what I came here for."
> Mr Mackenzie was afraid of the expression in her eyes. He
> thought, "My God, she's going to attack me. I ought to stop
> her."
> But, as it might have been in a nightmare, he could not do
> anything to stop her.
> Assault! Premeditation could be proved. She wouldn't get
> away with it – not even here in Paris.
> A cunning expression came into Julia's face. She picked up her
> glove and hit his cheek with it, but so lightly that he did not even
> blink.
> "I despise you," she said.
> "Quite," said Mr Mackenzie. He sat very straight, staring at
> her.

Again, the device of free indirect style plays an important part in
contributing to the total effect of the scene. The sense of anticlimax
when Julia lightly brushes Mackenzie's cheek with her glove is

only possible through the build-up of hysteria in his mind. The fine artistic control in the narrative arrangement where Mackenzie's exaggerated fears are undercut by the coolness of Julia's performance, makes this passage one of the most superb moments in the entire canon of Jean Rhys's writing. The perfection of the writing itself, however, is never allowed to overshadow the human pain which is both its content and its function to transcend. Thus, we are not allowed to forget that Julia's momentary triumph over Mackenzie is not wrought without personal suffering:

> Her eyes did not drop, but a mournful and beaten expression came into them.
> "Oh well," she said, "all right. Have it your own way."
> Then, to Mr Mackenzie's unutterable relief, she gathered up her gloves and walked out of the restaurant.

The expression of defeat in Julia's eyes comes from the recognition that despite the success of the moment, she can never really win. In her words 'Have it your own way', she registers that the Mackenzies of the world will always have it their own way, because of the way in which they have organised society. Consequently, Julia cannot hope to maintain her ascendancy over the likes of him for very long and, indeed, realising this, she takes the only option available to her – to submit by leaving the scene of the battle.

The insight into the consciousness of Julia's sister Norah is of great significance, not only because it provides us with a definite contrast to Julia, but also because she is a living reminder of what Julia herself might have become had she not made a decision to alter the pattern of her life. If we were to use Horsfield's words,[3] we might regard Norah as 'one of the others'. Unlike Mackenzie, however, Norah is a woman, and exists on very small financial means. For her, the effort to live the traditional life-style, to become a respectable member of society, has led to spiritual and physical impoverishment:

> Norah was labelled for all to see. She was labelled 'Middle class, no money.' Hardly enough to keep herself in clean linen.

And yet scrupulously, fiercely clean, but with all the daintiness perforce cut out. Everything about her betrayed the woman who has been brought up to certain tastes, then left without the money to gratify them; trained to certain opinions which forbid her even the relief of rebellion against her lot; yet holding desperately to both her tastes and her opinions. (p.53)

The contrast between such rigid conformity to middle-class values and the determination of chance which governs Julia's own way of life, is clearly seen when the latter cannot bring herself to explain her presence in London:

> Julia sat down on the bed and began: "I decided to come over very suddenly."
> Then she stopped. "If a car hoots before I count three, I'll do this. If it doesn't, I'll do that . . ." To know that this was the only reasonable way to live was one thing; to explain and justify it to somebody else – especially to Norah – was quite another. (p.51)

Such a lack of real communication characterises their relationship, for, despite Julia's 'longing' for the affection of her sister, Norah's own intransigence is unbending. The years of self-denial, during which she has felt obliged to nurse her ailing mother, have taken their toll and left her bereft of human warmth. This characteristic is most noticeable when she speaks: 'She had a sweet voice, a voice with a warm and tender quality. This was strange, because her face was cold, as though warmth and tenderness were dead in her.' The contradiction in her personality points towards the potential in her for genuine human feeling, and this makes the presence of so much bitterness in her life all the more pitiable. Norah is not depicted without sympathy. An extended inroad into her consciousness allows us to see her predicament from her own point of view. It occurs during Julia's first visit to the flat in Acton, where her mother lies dying. Sympathy for Norah begins with Wyatt's praises of her to Julia:

> "Norah's a good kid. . . . She's had a long time of this and I've never heard her grouse, never once. She's a good kid. And she'll be all right. She's young yet." (p.73)

Julia, herself, having witnessed her sister managing to calm her mother after the distress caused by her own visit, is moved to see Norah 'like a character in a tremendous tragedy moving, dark, tranquil, and beautiful, across a background of yellowish snow.' For the first time, the two of them are able to talk about their common background, although Norah's defensive attitude prevents any development of intimacy, by bringing the initial warmth which is elicited to an abrupt end:

> ... Norah said with a half-laugh: "Well, we've neither of us done very well for ourselves, have we?"
> Julia lifted her shoulders, as if to say: "Well, don't ask me."
> "The fact is," said Norah, "that there's something wrong with our family. We're soft or lazy, or something."
> "I don't think you are lazy," said Julia. "And I shouldn't say that you were too soft, either."
> She spoke gently, but Norah felt suddenly breathless, as if they were on the verge of a quarrel. She muttered: "No, I don't think I'm soft now. . . . Perhaps I'm not very soft now." (p.74)

We recall that on their earlier meeting it had been Julia who had desperately wanted to communicate with Norah, on the level of their family tie alone if nothing else:

> She wanted to say: "Do you remember the day I took off my shoes and stockings when we were paddling and carried you because the pebbles hurt your feet? Well, I've never forgotten that day." (p.52)

The contrast between this reminiscence and the content of Norah's utterance above does pinpoint the emotional difference between them, with Norah only able to measure success in terms of social standing. Julia's desire to achieve real communication on a human level is quite foreign to her sister whose comment demonstrates her inability to value the warmth of human intercourse for its own sake.

Now, with Julia's assertion that she is not 'too soft' forcing the younger woman to examine herself, the alteration of narrative level to Norah's point of view occurs. Initially, the tone adopted is that of a fierce indignation which is stimulated, no doubt, by a feeling of personal slight as a result of what she has taken to be an unjust critical comment:

> She felt a tightness of the throat, and her eyes stung. She opened
> them widely, and leaned her head back, because she knew that if
> she did that the tears would not fall; they would go back to
> wherever they came from. She did not want to give herself away
> before Julia – Julia with her hateful, blackened eyelids. What was
> the use of telling Julia what she thought of her? It was ridiculous
> to make a scene. You ignored people like that. (p.74)

The movement into free indirect style here narrows the distance
and effects collusion between the reader and the character so that
our sympathy for Norah is increased. Her alternative view of Julia
is important, making for a more balanced portrait of the main
character than was achieved in *Quartet*. However, the extravagance
of Norah's attack does modify our sympathy a little – we take her
use of 'hateful' and 'blackened' to be evidence of an overwrought
mind, and her fear of making 'a scene' connects her with Mackenzie. Certainly, his view of Julia may be sensed in Norah's own
dismissive reference to 'people like that'. Despite this link, Norah
is treated with more understanding than Mackenzie was. A return
to the less emotional third-person mode makes some attempt to
account rationally for her negative feelings:

> And yet every time she looked at Julia she felt a fierce desire to
> hurt her or to see her hurt and humiliated. She thought in a
> confused way, "It's because I'm so tired." All day she had felt
> like that, as if she could not bear another instant. When she had
> held a spoon of medicine to her mother's lips her hand had
> shaken so violently that it had been all spilled. And all last night
> she had lain awake thinking, instead of sleeping, now that Wyatt
> was there, and she had a chance to sleep. She had lain awake
> thinking and crying – and to cry was a thing she hardly ever did.

Norah's own explanation of her attitude to Julia in terms of her
'tiredness' is insufficient to account for the depth of her hostility.
The desire to inflict pain upon another person as a mark of one's
contempt for them betrays a deep-seated neurosis which may not
so easily be accounted for. Rather more likely as a cause is the
injustice of her own oppressed position within society, subconsciously felt if not consciously stated. A comparison between her
lot and Julia's relative freedom from such bonds is much more
likely to result in the degree of resentment which she displays: 'It

was as if meeting Julia had aroused some spirit of rebellion to tear her to bits. She thought over and over again, "It isn't fair, it isn't fair."' The contrast between the two women is, perhaps, most deeply felt in Norah's admission, at the end of the section, that despite the negativity of the feelings aroused in her by Julia's presence, they do at least have some positive effect:

> "I'll come to the door with you," said Norah. She now felt that she did not want to let Julia go. She hated her, but she felt more alive when her sister was with her. (p.77)

The irony of this situation is an implicit indictment of the social structure which allows such hatred to be generated by such oppression. On a personal level too, it is at this point that we sympathise most with Norah who knows that she is alive only when thus stimulated to negative feelings of enmity and jealousy.

Her own method of dealing with these frustrations is seen in her tendency to wallow in self-pity. This neither makes her any more appetising a creature, nor helps her to combat her oppression positively. Her allusion to a weakness in the family is thus felt to be quite appropriate. The inclination is most strongly suggested in the passage which develops as she recalls her sleeplessness of the previous night:

> She picked up the book lying on her bed-table – *Almayer's Folly* – and had begun to read:

>> The slave had no hope, and knew of no change. She knew of no other sky, no other water, no other forest, no other world, no other life. She had no wish, no hope, no love. . . . The absence of pain and hunger was her happiness, and when she felt unhappy she was tired, more than usual, after the day's labour. (pp.74–5)

The allusion here makes plain the link between the oppressed slave and Norah's own position. Certainly, Norah herself would feel that link to be justified, and it is likely that her choice of the book arises from that very recognition. The fact that the lack of any narrative comment on this particular selection of reading matter is not felt, demonstrates its very transparency. It also suggests, however, a certain narrative sympathy for Norah, whose faults are allowed to stand alone with no ironic mediation by a textual voice keen to render her failings comic. This soft treatment is a privilege

accorded to Norah alone – Mackenzie, as we have seen, does not
escape without some narrative cutting down to size. Clearly, the
sympathetic treatment for one of 'the others' demonstrates that the
issue is not as clear-cut as Horsfield had implied. Norah's situation
is a reminder of what Julia herself might have become had she not
made the break.

The analepsis continues in a compassionate vein. Norah sees the
reality of the situation when she looks at herself in the mirror. The
unfulfilled sexual potential of her body fills her with frustration:

> She had let the nightgown slip down off her shoulders, and had
> a look at herself. She was tall and straight and slim and young –
> well, fairly young. She had taken up a strand of her hair and put
> her face against it and thought how she liked the smell and the
> feel of it. She had laughed at herself in the glass and her teeth
> were white and sound and even. Yes she had laughed at herself
> in the glass. Like an idiot.
>
> Then in the midst of her laughter she had noticed how pale
> her lips were; and she had thought: "My life's like death. It's like
> being buried alive." (p.75)

We respond sympathetically to this erotic description of her hair,
and the pathos of the scene is increased on her recognition of her
own existence as a living death.

Set against the latent feminity of Norah, and standing as a threat
to its full development, is the ever-present shadow of Miss Wyatt.
There is an overt suggestion of butch lesbianism in the masculinity
of the posture which she adopts:

> Her brown hair was cut very short, drawn away from a high,
> narrow forehead, and brushed to lie close to her very small skull.
> Her nose was thin and arched. She had small, pale-brown eyes
> and a determined expression. She wore a coat and skirt of grey
> flannel, a shirt blouse, and a tie. (p.68)

Such style, together with her partiality for 'Navy Cut tobacco' and
her 'gestures of a man', clearly indicate her position in the
household as something of an antecedent 'Sister George'.
Obviously, she exercises greater influence over Norah than merely
advising her on medical matters and assisting her with the nursing
of her mother. Norah's reluctance to turn her out in favour of her

sister when Julia asks if she might stay at the flat during her brief visit to London, is a clear indication of this; so too, is Wyatt's protective manner towards Norah, and her overt disapproval of Julia. Her function in the novel is to add to our sympathy for Norah, whom we see not only as being trapped in a situation which is stultifying, but also, even in her choice of friends, finding no possible means of developing her potential to the fullest.

The rigidity of Wyatt's opinions, and by contrast the malleability of Norah, is appreciated most in their final scene together, after the departure of Julia, when the impression of the younger woman which we are left with is again a sympathetic one. Immediately following the death of her mother, a change in Norah's attitude is shown by the manner in which she squeezes her sister's arm:

> Norah was very tired and sad, but behind her sadness was a rested feeling which made her feel gentle and pitiful to every-one, even for the moment to Julia. It was as if the hard core of her heart was melted. (p.90)

The reconciliation which this seems to anticipate, however, never develops. Instead, following the funeral, Julia's inability to contain her contempt for the hypocrisy of the 'respectable' results in a full-scale slanging match when Norah, again on the defensive, takes her sister's comments personally. This widens the chasm between the two women, destroying any possibility of the estab-lishment of harmony. Significantly, following this, it is Wyatt who adopts the dominant role and effectively removes Julia from the flat. The excuse with which she rationalises this manoeuvre is the protection of Norah who 'has been through enough'. But the likelihood is that, standing to benefit indirectly from Norah's mother's will,[4] she fears the possible consequences of any intru-sion on Julia's part. Reconciliation between the two sisters, there-fore, is not in Wyatt's interests.

Despite the preceding altercation, Norah herself becomes anx-ious for her sister's welfare when she realises that Julia has gone:

> Norah was sitting up on the sofa. She said: "Where's Julia?"
>
> "She's gone home," answered Miss Wyatt. "Much better for her."
>
> "Oh, no," said Norah in a hysterical voice. "We can't send her away like that. I don't believe she's got any money."

"My dear," said Miss Wyatt, "just you lie down and keep yourself still. Your sister's going to write."

"Oh," said Norah.

"Of course," said Miss Wyatt with contempt. "She'll write." (pp.100–1)

The "contempt" in Wyatt's voice forms a distinct contrast to the fearfulness in Norah's, and the full control of the situation which the older woman displays is a little disconcerting. A moment of insight into the turmoil of Norah's own mind further demonstrates her vulnerability, and seen thus against the background of Wyatt's cool intransigence, it evokes our sympathy:

Norah lay back, with her eyes shut. She thought: "My God, how hard I've got!" Her lips trembled. "What's happened to me?" For a moment she was afraid of herself. (p.101)

Even this instant of self-knowledge is tempered by Wyatt's ministrations:

Presently she heard from the kitchen the rattling noise of tea-cups in saucers. A feeling of rest crept from her knees upwards to her eyes. The clock ticked: "You're young yet – young yet – young yet."

The 'feeling of rest' which is engendered is in direct contrast to the sense of urgency which the ticking of the clock would normally convey. The comforting sound issuing from the kitchen where Wyatt has commenced her take-over lulls Norah into a false sense of security, making her misinterpret the ominous sound of the clock. Thus, failing to appreciate the symbolic link between the transience of her youth and the relentlessness of time passing, she bestows upon its workings a reassuring message that she is still young enough to make a life for herself.

Set in ironic juxtaposition to Norah's mistaken sense of leisure, is a view of Julia walking along the street, from Uncle Griffiths' point of view:

As she walked she jerked herself from side to side, in the manner of a woman who is tired and no longer young walking on very high heels. People turned round to look at her. (p.101)

This sudden alteration of focus allows the chapter to end on a portentous note which not only demonstrates the pathetic effect on Julia of Norah and Wyatt's combined cruelty, but also suggests that Norah's turn to grow old may come sooner than she thinks. Uncle Griffiths' deliberate avoidance of his niece, crossing 'over to the other side of the street' rather than confronting her, is the final gesture of abandonment which Julia will suffer at the hands of her family. From this point in the diegesis, there will be no further contact with any of them, and our realisation of this adds to the pathos of the image of the lonely woman making her way down the street.

It is the complexity of this image, and the complexity of our response to it – the fact that we do not really know what to make of Julia – that is the sign of the development in Rhys's art. Norah's position in the social system complicates rather than simplifies our response to Julia, and adds to the difficulty of reading her. Clearly, Norah is one of 'the others'. As we have seen, she herself identifies with the likes of Mackenzie. The irony is, however, that she is a woman, and, as such, is oppressed by the very patriarchy which men like Mackenzie represent. She lives the system without trying to combat it, and is critical of Julia's attempts to better her lot. But society has made Norah bitter and full of self-pity. Clearly, the negativity of her portrait in the novel, as well as the compassion with which it is drawn, is an authorial indictment of the very system which has made the character what she is, and which she herself blindly upholds.

The third-person narrative mode which has allowed such scope for alternative views of Julia to be developed, is dropped in favour of the first-person stance in Rhys's third novel, *Voyage in the Dark*. I should now like to examine how this shift in mode makes for a deeper penetration of the consciousness of the main character, allowing us to appreciate psychological complexities which account, to a certain extent, for her acute sense of alienation and detachment from the society in which she lives. Anna Morgan is far too sensitive a creature to be able to make a success of using her potential as a woman to exploit men. Her attempt to do so is shown to contribute to her own sense of her existence as nothing more than a living death.

4
Anna's Darkness

The use of the 'I narrator' in *Voyage in the Dark* is, perhaps, a logical technical development. It may be seen to arise out of that tendency towards making such a close identification of the third-person narrative voice with the point of view of the main character, which we observed both in *Quartet* and *After Leaving Mr Mackenzie*. This particular narrative situation, however, demands that the complexities of Anna's personality be conveyed through her own voice itself, without access to any alternative perspectives. These complexities emerge incidentally as her discourse develops; they are implied through the way in which she engages herself with the world and with the other people whom she meets. But that engagement is not a happy one, and in this chapter I should like to focus on the development of certain structures of meaning which suggest that her personality is at odds with the world in which she lives, and that a deep-seated sense of alienation and detachment, characterised by an increasing withdrawal into herself, blights her ability to relate to other people in a positive way. In this respect, Anna may be seen to differ radically from Marya who, as we have appreciated, is affected more by particular circumstances in her life than by her perception of the world. She also differs in a significant way from Julia whom we see at the advance of middle age and whose neurosis, therefore, may strike us as having been shaped by the personal experiences which she has collected over the years. With Anna, a younger 'Rhys woman' than either of her predecessors, there is a suggestion that it is her potential for a sense of personal isolation which lies at the root of her difficulties with developing positive human relationships.

The first-person narrative stance suggests the propensity of the main character for story-telling. It also raises the question of reliability and brings with it a particular problem for the reader. By what standard are we to judge the story which Anna tells of her view of herself and the world in which she lives? These are issues which are given an implicit focus very early in the novel, and they are worth considering not only for the insight which they bring into Anna's character, but also for the question which they raise about her status as a fictional creation. As the novel develops, we will see Anna's sense of her engagement with the world troubling her sufficiently for her to withdraw into the recesses of her own imagination. On the level of the discourse too, there is a corresponding withdrawal, when the reader's own apprehension of Anna's identity is challenged by certain textual structures which work towards obliterating her image as a living human being from our immediate focus.

The central irony of the text itself – a text which has been created out of the mind of a fictional character – is implied in a fascinating descriptive passage which corresponds to a pause in the conversation between Anna and her friend, Maudie Beardon, in the first chapter of the novel:

> I was lying on the sofa, reading *Nana*. It was a paper-covered book with a coloured picture of a stout, dark woman brandishing a wine-glass. She was sitting on the knee of a bald-headed man in evening dress. The print was very small, and the endless procession of words gave me a curious feeling – sad, excited and frightened. It wasn't what I was reading, it was the look of the dark, blurred words going on endlessly that gave me that feeling. (p.9)

A link between the central character of Zola's novel and our own narrator suggests itself not only by the similarity of situation – Nana's connection with the theatre and her fall into prostitution foreshadow Anna's career and moral decline – but also by the anagrammatism which Rhys seems to have practised in the choice of a name for her protagonist.[1] The subject of prostitution itself is broached through suggestion rather than direct reference. The fact that the illustration on the cover of the book is described in such detail implies that it has a particular significance which Rhys wishes to draw attention to. But, characteristically, it is left to the reader to determine any interpretation of its visual meaning. In fact, the narrator attempts to deflect attention away from the content of the book by focusing on the visual effect which the words themselves have on her. This is a clever manoeuvre on the part of the author, for the pointed nature of the gesture actually results in drawing even more attention to the cover, the symbolic value of which will be fully appreciated on a second reading. It also provides one of the clearest examples of the tension which exists between the 'narrating I' and the 'narrated I'. The effect achieved here is one of irony, felt especially in the statement – 'It wasn't what I was reading . . .' – and this is one of the means by which distance is achieved within this complex narrative mode. However, this emotional reaction to the print is not merely a narrative manoeuvre to effect distance through irony, it also foreshadows the protagonist's later intoxication with words, which will manifest itself in the reams she will scribble to Walter Jeffries on his termination of their affair.

With the resumption of the dialogue between the two women, the themes both of prostitution and the building of narratives are combined in a much more direct handling when the forthright and unsophisticated Maudie comes straight to the point:

> "I'll get dressed," Maudie said, "and then we'd better go out and get some air. We'll go to the theatre and see if there are any letters. That's a dirty book, isn't it?"
> "Bits of it are all right," I said.
> Maudie said, "I know; it's about a tart. I think it's disgusting. I bet you a man writing a book about a tart tells a lot of lies one way and another. Besides, all books are like that – just somebody stuffing you up."

The contrast between Maudie and Anna suggests itself in the former's brash manner of speaking, seen here and previously in her altercation with the landlady, and in Anna's relative taciturnity. This is the first instance of direct speech attributed to Anna in the text, and its non-commital laconicism will characterise all her future utterances. There is irony in this natural verbal reservation, for it belies her declared interest in words. But it does highlight the great difference between the unuttered word and the spoken, and Anna's leaning towards the former is accompanied by a withdrawal from a more direct engagement with speech.

Maudie's comments on authorial bias which can lead to 'a lot of lies' is interesting. Not only does it develop the theme of the written word, but it also casts doubt on the integrity of narratives. There is something anarchic in this idea, for the absolutes of truth which the naïve reader expects to find in the text are treated with scepticism. By implication, the status of *Voyage in the Dark*, the text under scrutiny, does not escape this modification. Through Maudie, Jean Rhys seems to be presenting a view of the text in general – 'all books' – which is subversive in its very uncertainty: does it reflect a truth? Is the question of 'somebody stuffing you up' a form of truth? Rhys ensures that the attention of her readers will be drawn to the import of Maudie's words by a clever manoeuvre to mislead them. Initially, the reader may misinterpret Maudie's sense of disgust, taking it to be a moralistic judgement on the behaviour of prostitutes. This judgement is immediately modified, however, when we realise that she expresses, rather, a sense of indignation that the case of the 'tart' will not have been put forward accurately. Now, in the physical description of Maudie which follows, the implications of her sense of injustice are brought out, for there is a strong suggestion that she herself could identify with the prostitute:

> Maudie was tall and thin, and her nose made a straight line with her forehead. She had pale yellow hair and a very white, smooth skin. When she smiled a tooth was missing on one side. She was twenty-eight years old and all sorts of things had happened to her. She used to tell me about them when we came back from the theatre at night. "You've only got to learn how to swank a bit, then you're all right," she would say. Lying in bed with her, her hair in two long yellow plaits on either side of her long white face.
> "Swank's the word," she would say.

The most significant feature of Maudie's appearance is her missing tooth. Attention is drawn to it because of its unusualness. We may recognise a literary counterpart in Chaucer's 'gap-toothed' Wife of Bath. In medieval times the characteristic signified lecherousness, and this quality is borne out in Alison's tale of her promiscuity. In *Voyage in the Dark*, the irony evident in the line immediately following the mention of this detail does seem to point to some sexual significance. But in her characteristically understated style, Rhys does not dwell on the details, preferring to allow readers to make what they will out of the innuendoes. Thus, the only remnant of Maudie's 'tale' to be salvaged in the text is her advice to Anna to learn how to 'swank'.

Not only the missing tooth, but the plaited hair and 'white smooth skin' conjure up a picture which is essentially medieval in

tone. The blonde hair too, is a feature stereotypically associated
with the beauties of the Middle Ages. Yet there is ambiguity in the
colour 'yellow' which draws attention to itself through repetition.
Echoing the description of the 'grey-yellow' light outside (p.9), the
colour has an association with age and a loss of purity. This,
together with the repetition of 'long' in the description of Maudie's
hair and face as she lies in bed tempers the image of her with a hint
of the comic.

Maudie's extrovert personality is important, for her function in
this first chapter is not only to give Anna the benefit of her advice
on the subject of attracting men, but also to provide a practical
example of it, and in doing so effect an introduction between the
younger girl and Walter Jeffries. No doubt, left to her own devices,
Anna would have shied away from any attempt on the part of a
stranger to engage her in conversation, and thus there would have
been no novel. It is Maudie who assesses the potential in the two
men who follow them in the street, recognises that they are
well-off, and therefore encourages them in their efforts to 'get off
with' both her and Anna. She it is who keeps the conversation
going with her corny jokes, and invites them back to the lodgings
for 'tea'. And, indeed, it is through this situation that we learn a
little more background detail about the narrator herself, for, in
Maudie's comically theatrical introduction of themselves to Jones
and Jeffries, at last we are given the name of our protagonist: '. . .
allow me to introduce Miss Anna Morgan and Miss Maudie
Beardon, now appearing in *The Blue Waltz* . . .'

Throughout the duration of the interchange between the four of
them, Anna remains subdued, answering questions when asked,
but never, herself, initiating a topic of conversation, and unable to
appreciate the light-heartedness of the banter. Increasingly, she
experiences a sense of detachment from what is going on around
her, distancing herself from it through the affectation of hatred and
scorn for the whole process of 'picking up people'. Indeed, it is
only through the liberating influence of alcohol that she is able to
join in at all, although even then she experience a curious sense of
detachment by observing the reflection of herself in a mirror:

> I hated them both. You pick up people and then they are rude
> to you. This business of picking up people and then they always
> imagine they can be rude to you.
> But when I had had a glass of port I began to laugh too and

after that I couldn't stop. I watched myself in the glass over the mantelpiece, laughing. (p.12)

This is the first of many references to mirrors in the novel, and a full discussion of their significance will be undertaken in due course. For the moment, 'the glass' acts as a distancing device, allowing Anna to detach herself from the real experience and view it at a remove. So remote does she appear to be in the company, that Maudie even begins to talk about her in the third-person, as though she were not there:

> "She's always cold," Maudie said. "She can't help it. She was born in a hot place. She was born in the West Indies or somewhere, weren't you kid? The girls call her the Hottentot. Isn't it a shame?"

Again, Maudie's words are of more significance than she realises. Through the term 'Hottentot', Anna's sense of alienation is emphasised, her formative years having been spent abroad. However, I suggest that the estrangement which she feels is not due merely to this difference of background, but is rather because of a sensitivity which sets her apart from the people with whom she mixes. This awareness, or perceptiveness, makes Anna's sensibility exceptional. In this chapter, for instance, there is a moment when she is moved almost to tears on comparing the sound of a piano which she hears by chance to that made by a waterfall:

> Somebody was playing the piano in one of the houses we passed – a tinkling sound like water running. I began to walk very slowly because I wanted to listen. But it got farther and farther away and then I couldn't hear it any more. "Gone for ever," I thought. There was a tight feeling in my throat as if I wanted to cry. (p.10)

The nostalgic association of the 'water running' with the sound of streams tumbling down the mountains in her West Indian homeland may well account for the emotion which she feels. But the suggestion is left open, the link does not become definite, and this ambiguity adds to the touching ephemerality of the moment of experience. Perhaps there is no reason to explain the 'tight feeling' which is elicited other than the sheer beauty of the moment. What is clear from this heightened awareness, however, is that Anna is no ordinary eighteen-year-old. Maudie's only direct reference to her as 'kid', therefore, has an ironic effect. The term emphasises her considerable youth, she is ten years younger than Maudie, and thus it adds to Anna's sense of alienation from the others. But the odd effect of its application draws attention to the uniqueness of her way of seeing: Anna is no ordinary 'kid' either.

Anna's lack of experience does reveal itself in her response to Walter Jeffries, however. Not realising the significance for him of picking up a strange girl in a down-market seaside resort, she mistakenly senses a respect for herself where there is none:

> He spoke very quickly, but with each word separated from the other. He didn't look at my breasts or my legs, as they usually do. Not that I saw. He looked straight at me and listened to everything I said with a polite and attentive expression, and then he looked away and smiled as if he had sized me up. (p.12)

Later, Walter's behaviour is put into perspective when he becomes embarrassed by his cousin, Vincent, teasing him.[2] For the moment, however, he treats Anna with studied care, having assessed her lack of experience, and fearful lest he frighten her off. He has already seen the immaturity of her indignation on the question of doubt about her age – 'I can show you my birth certificate if you like' – and this has intrigued him. His companion, Jones, speaks with condescending irony when he declines the offer of proof: 'No, my dear child, no. That would be excessive,' – but, for Jeffries, Anna's behaviour smacks of virginity and represents a sexual challenge which he is keen to take up.

The issue of virginity is touched on a little later in the chapter, when the two women are alone, in a revealing moment of daydreaming which Anna indulges in in preference to paying attention to Maudie's incessant chatter. This is a good example of Anna's inclination to remove herself mentally from what is going on around her, and to substitute memory for real human inter-course. It is a lesson in detachment:

> She went on talking about him. I didn't listen.
> Thinking how cold the street would be outside and the dressing-room cold too, and that my place was by the door in the draught. It always was. A damned shame. And about Laurie

Gaynor, who was dressing next me that week. The virgin, she calls me, or sometimes the silly cow. ("Can't you manage to keep the door shut, Virgin, you silly cow?") But I like her better than any of the others. She's a fine girl. She's the only one I really like. And the cold nights; and the way my collar-bones stick out in my first-act dress. There's something you can buy that makes your neck fat. Venus Carnis. "No fascination without curves. Ladies, realize your charms." But it costs three guineas and where can I get three guineas? And the cold nights, the damned cold nights. (p.15)

The introduction to Laurie Gaynor here is important, for it is through this new character that the theme of virginity is opened up. Her affectionately contemptuous labelling of Anna brings out that quality which the experienced Walter Jeffries had sensed in the younger girl. Its emphasis on her sexual innocence also confirms her alienation from the fellow members of the chorus, making her stand out among them, on the receiving-end of their jibes. The cruelty practised in the dressing-room is not tackled directly, but it is suggested in Anna's pathetic attachment to Laurie who is 'the only one' of the entire troupe whom she really likes. In this way, through the innocent irony in her voice, the narrating Anna can command our sympathy for the narrated Anna, as much by what she does not say as by what is actually uttered. No doubt it is the feeling of self-consciousness elicited by Anna's rough treatment at the hands of her fellows which leads her to consider the imperfections of her neck. Possibly this has been the subject of some banter in the past, and there is much pathos in her anticipation of finding a cosmetic to cover it up.

In the paragraph following this, which is stimulated by a contrast with the idea of the 'cold', we may locate the origins of Anna's disillusionment with her present lot in life:

Lying between 15°10′ and 15°40′N. and 61°14′ and 61°30′W. "A goodly island and something highland, but all overgrown with weeds," that book said. And all crumpled into hills and mountains as you would crumple a piece of paper in your hand – rounded green hills and sharply-cut mountains.

This is the second strand in a West Indian tapestry which was initiated by the first paragraph in the novel.[3] Now, the location becomes more precisely identified with Jean Rhys's own birthplace of Dominica when the geographical indication of its position on the globe is given.[4] The quotation from the guidebook which complements these statistics gives a broader, more panoramic view of the terrain, and focuses particularly on a characteristic of wild fecundity. The Shakespearean tone established by the epithet 'goodly', however, has a curious irony, for, applied as it is to an island, it conjures up an association with Prospero's exotic place of exile. There, Miranda first met Ferdinand, and innocently applied the term to all who hailed from that 'brave new world' in Europe.[5] The reality of Anna's own 'brave new world' of England falls far short of a similarly idealistic anticipation of it which she had had ever since, as a child, she had been able to read about it in books:

> A curtain fell and then I was here.
> ... This is England Hester said and I watched it through the train-window divided into squares like pocket-handkerchiefs; a small tidy look it had everywhere fenced off from everywhere else – what are those things – those are haystacks – oh those are haystacks – I had read about England ever since I could read – smaller meaner everything is never mind – this is London – hundreds thousands of white people white people rushing along and the dark houses all alike frowning down one after the other all alike all stuck together – the streets like smooth shut-in ravines and the dark houses frowning down – oh I'm not going to like this place I'm not going to like this place I'm not going to like this place – you'll get used to it Hester kept saying I expect you feel like a fish out of water but you'll soon get used to it – now don't look like Dying Dick and Solemn Davy as your poor father used to say you'll get used to it ... (pp.15–16)

Now, the significance of the image of the crumpled paper may be seen, and I suggest that it reveals in Anna a curious ambivalence of feeling for her island home. The act of destroying a piece of paper, such as a page from a book, by crumpling it in one's hand, implies that it is no longer of value, either because it has served its purpose or because the information on it is misleading. Thus, for whichever reason, the description of Dominica in 'that book' might suffer, as might the pages in the reference books which had promised such a different England. That Anna applies the same term 'crumpled' to her memory of the 'hills and mountains' of Dominica implies that she has modified her view of them, although the clarity of 'rounded green hills and sharply-cut mountains' with which the memory ends is in distinct opposition to this view. Perhaps, then, her attempt to destroy the memory is unsuccessful, so deeply ingrained is it on her imagination.

Looking again at the image of England which is stimulated by the memory of the 'goodly island' immediately preceding it, we notice that the impressions of each place are divided by a return to the idea of the 'curtain' with which the text had opened. Now, though, instead of the vagueness of approach inherent in the preamble to the simile – 'it was as if a' – there is a much more precise use of metaphor which makes the separation more distinct – 'A curtain fell' – and adds to the sense of an abrupt jolt brought about by a sudden awareness of the culture shock – 'and then I was here'.[6]

A significant technical feature which is noticeable in this passage is the unusual presentation of direct speech. Hester's utterances are deprived of their quotation marks and become woven into the text without any typographical demarcation of their limits. In such a form they become part of Anna's own mental construction, undifferentiated from those thoughts which originate within her own mind, and this is indicative of the depth of her level of abstraction at this point. Indeed, it is likely that the ellipsis marks at the beginning of this passage are intended to signify an alteration in the level of her consciousness. This signal will be repeated only when Anna's moment of abstraction is interrupted by Maudie, whereupon she will return to the level demanded by an actual verbal exchange with another human being.

A further technical feature to be observed is the method by which Rhys manages to convey the actual rhythm of the train's wheels as it runs over the tracks. This is accomplished by the three-fold repetition of Anna's negative utterance: 'I'm not going to like this place I'm not going to like this place I'm not gong to like this place.' It is unlikely that she actually utters the words in such rapid succession in the diegesis, although it is clear from Hester's answer that she does give voice to the feeling at least once: '. . . you'll get used to it.' No doubt, finding that her utterance fits the rhythm of the train, it becomes fixed in Anna's mind as the journey continues. Thus, at this point the text reflects the repetition of unexpressed thought, whereas in Hester's case the balancing three-fold repetition of her utterance is more likely to coincide with the actual number of times she 'kept saying it'.

The use of imagery in this passage is interesting too, for it reflects a stifling moral consciousness which Anna finds apparent in British culture everywhere. By a curious textual irony, the restraint imposed upon the English countryside with its 'tidy look' is at odds with the technical licence adopted in the presentation of this view. Implicitly, this anticipates the difficulty which the mind perceiving it will have in coming to terms with such a rigid way of life. Here the hay is regimented into 'stacks', the fields are 'divided into squares', and the comparison with 'pocket-handkerchiefs' is an original one which aptly suggests the etiquette of the society. There is a fascinating effect of depersonalisation in the sheer number of 'hundreds thousands of white people . . . rushing along' who, thus presented, appear to be more like ants than human beings; and a transfer of the human characteristic of 'frowning', an expression of disapproval, to the houses, adds to a growing sense of oppression inherent in the very architecture of the nation. Faced with the prospect of living in the gaze of such disapproval, it is hardly surprising that the young Anna should adopt the aspect of 'Dying Dick and Solemn Davy'. Clearly, her first impressions of England fall short of her expectations.

Towards the end of the chapter the use of ellipsis makes for a considerable increase in the pace of the text so that two weeks of diegetic duration are compressed into a mere four or five lines:

> "Only three more weeks of this damned tour, T.G.," Maudie said. "It's no life, not in winter it isn't."
>
> When we were coming home from the theatre that night it began to rain and in Brighton it rained all the time. We got to Holloway and it was winter and the dark streets round the theatre made me think of murders. (p.16)

The nature of this textual compression suggests that the motivating interest of the novel is Anna's developing relationship with Jeffries. He having returned to London, there is no further potential for textual development until in the diegesis Anna herself arrives in the city. The use of ellipsis, therefore, allows the text to omit the rest of her time in Southsea, and the entire week in Brighton, in order that the chapter may be completed with the focus on an invitation which she has received from Walter:

I gave Maudie the letter to read and she said, "I told you so. I told you he had money. That's an awfully swanky club. The four swankiest clubs in London are . . ."

All the girls started arguing about which was the swankiest club in London. (pp.16–17)

With deliberate narrative economy, Walter Jeffries is thus reintroduced into the text. The circumstances surrounding Anna's receipt of the letter are not given, and there is no direct naming of the sender. It is left to Maudie's comments to identify him, which they do implicitly. The narrative abandonment of her sentence in mid-utterance, and the summary of the subsequent utterance, again speed up the pace of the text, thus emphasising the importance of Anna's relationship with Walter. The focus falls instead on a narratisation of her written reply, and here we are given clear evidence of the potential for unreliability which narratives possess:

I wrote and said I couldn't dine with him on Monday, because I had a previous engagement. ("Always say you have a previous engagement.") But I said I could dine on Wednesday, the 17th. of November, and I gave him the address of the room I had taken in Judd Street.

Implicit within the textual arrangement of this paragraph is a suggestion of Anna's immaturity. This is seen not only in her ready acceptance of the advice in the bracketed quotation, but also in her child-like report of the exact date of the proposed meeting. Usually, in a summary such as this narratisation of her letter, such detail would be omitted and a less precise reference substituted. No doubt, for Anna, this day will remain significant for the rest of her life. As far as we are concerned, however, our memory of the deftness with which Walter accomplished his seduction of her earlier in the diegesis now works to evoke our sympathy for the girl who, we feel, prepares thus to meet her fate like a lamb to the slaughter. And our misgivings are not allayed by the ambiguous note upon which the chapter ends:

Laurie Gaynor said, "Tell him to borrow the club tin-opener. Say "P.S. Don't forget the tin-opener."

"Oh, leave her alone," Maudie said.

"That's all right," Laurie said. "I'm not troubling her. I'm teaching her etiquette."

"She knows I'm a good old cow," Laurie said. "A lot better than most of the other old cows. Aren't I, what's-your-name-Anna?"

Laurie Gaynor's act of naming Anna is important for two reasons. Firstly, the hesitant manner in which the approach is made draws attention to the name itself, which reminds us of our earlier suspicion that its significance is linked anagrammatically to 'Nana'. This echo, then, re-evokes the idea of prostitutes in our minds. Secondly, and linked with this ominous suggestion, the alteration of Laurie's address from 'Virgin' to 'Anna' may be seen to be a symbolic anticipation of the loss of sexual innocence which will follow the younger girl's involvement with Walter Jeffries. Thus, through textual relations, symbolic suggestion, and the play of innuendo, a wealth of meaning inheres in a few short lines. The narrative economy with which this richness is achieved is quite remarkable.

The theme of virginity is brought to its logical conclusion quite early in the novel, on only the second occasion of Anna's dining with Walter.[7] This time, their return to his house after the meal signifies a new approach on Walter's part after the aborted attempt during the previous opportunity in the suite at the Hoffner Hotel. Having learned from the mistake of his premature advances, he now carefully broaches the subject of virginity by way of introduction:

Then he started talking about my being a virgin and it all went – the feeling of being on fire – and I was cold.

"Why did you start about that?" I said. "What's it matter? Besides, I'm not a virgin if that's what's worrying you."

"You oughtn't to tell lies about that."

"I'm not telling lies, but it doesn't matter, anyway," I said. "People have made all that up."

"Oh yes, it matters. It's the only thing that matters."

"It's not the only thing that matters," I said. "All that's made up."

He stared at me and then he laughed. "You're quite right," he said. (pp.31–2)

The effect on Anna of such a clinical approach is similar to the effect which England has on her psyche. The 'cold' which she feels does not always relate to temperature but rather, as here, to an emotional state. Thus, her fear of the actual process of losing her virginity translates into a frigidity which manifests itself in lies and argumentativeness. But added to this is her genuine fear of seeming unsophisticated before Walter, which, ironically, leads her to make a gauche response and demonstrates the very quality which she had hoped to conceal. Walter's attitude remains patronising throughout, and this emphasises the gap between their respective states of maturity, with he attempting first to chide her for her untruthfulness and then to placate her by humouring her as though she were a child. His effort to stand corrected, however, does nothing to alleviate the tension which Anna feels:

> But I felt cold, as if someone had thrown cold water over me. When he kissed me I began to cry.
> "I must go," I thought. "Where's the door? I can't see the door. What's happened?" It was as if I were blind. (p.32)

This is a most significant moment, for the simile of blindness, used here to describe Anna's floundering in the face of a new experience, aptly conjures up the idea of darkness which is reflected in the title of the novel. The journey which Anna undergoes to reach a state of self-knowledge is made in total darkness. We have already appreciated the innocence of the 'narrated I'; now, though, that innocence takes on a symbolic quality which has ominous implications. A voyage in the dark is a hazardous affair; the prospect of reaching the destination must remain in doubt, and this uncertainty hangs over the entire text, bestowing, for us, a sense of futility on all of Anna's actions, in anticipation of their leading nowhere.

This sense of blindness which characterises Anna's actions is reflected in the text in several different ways. Firstly, it is seen in her reliance on other people to lead her. The notice which she takes of the advice of friends has already been observed; now it is Walter's turn to act as a guide, and he does so expertly, in spite of her feeble protestations:

> He wiped my eyes very gently with my handkerchief, but I kept saying, "I must go, I must go." Then we were going up

another flight of stairs and I walked softly. *"Crawling up the stairs
at three o'clock in the morning,"* she said. *Well I'm crawling up the
stairs.*

I stopped. I wanted to say, "No, I've changed my mind." But
he laughed and squeezed my hand and said, "What's the
matter? Come on, be brave," and I didn't say anything, but I felt
cold and as if I were dreaming.

A paternalistic role which he had adopted earlier when he had
attended to Anna's needs as she lay ill in her room,[8] is repeated in
his gentle wiping away of her tears. The impotence of her dissent is
suggested textually by the use of the imperfect tense to express the
lack of resistence met, in the sentence: 'Then we were going up
another flight of stairs and I walked softly.' This leads, by association, to a quotation of her landlady's words[9] which seem, in this
instance, to have been prophetic. But the sheer inevitability of
Anna's compliance is met in her adaptation of these words to
furnish an observation about her present action: *'Well, I'm crawling
up the stairs.'* The momentary alteration of tense to the present is
interesting, for it evokes a sense of universality about the action,
suggesting that the act of going to bed with a man, once undertaken, will be repeated to become a set pattern of life which the
'narrating I', herself, is still subject to. Thus, the use of the present
tense is anticipatory here when, briefly dropping the retrospective
mode of the narrative, it brings the level of the diegesis right up to
date with the time of writing.

The idea of 'dreaming' which is expressed in the simile at the
end of the above extract may be connected with the concept of
blindness in the respect of the dislocating effect which both states
have on the powers of orientation of the individual. We have
already observed the dislocating effect in the text itself which,
through a variation in the use of tense, modifies the main temporal
distance of the narrative, making the diegesis, for a moment,
simultaneous with the time of writing. But a new sense of
dislocation is achieved in actual narrative blind spots, and in the
use of language of uncertain reference, both of which make for
ambiguity. This is a second major way in which the sense of
blindness is reflected in the text, and it is most apparent in the
manner in which the sex act, itself, is treated:

When I got into bed there was warmth coming from him and I

got close to him. *Of course you've always known, always remembered, and then you forget so utterly, except that you've always known it. Always – how long is always?* (p.32)

Apart from the positive associations with the idea of 'warmth' which, in Anna's consciousness, always conjures up memories of her tropical background, there is nothing here to account for the effect of the experience to follow. Indeed, any reference to it is wiped out when the diegesis is abandoned after the first sentence. Instead, there is an alteration of narrative level which, like the quotation and adaptation of it analysed in the previous extract, is indicated typographically through the use of italics. This textual signal makes the ensuing change in tack stand out. Again, as previously, the temporal distance is affected when, this time, the use of 'you' points to an act of collusion between the 'narrating I' and the reader. In this way, a suggestion of universality is achieved, while at the same time the lack of certain reference in the language clouds the point, thus rendering the significance ambiguous. The textual effect of this passage is quite subversive. What Jean Rhys seems to be doing is, on the one hand, suggesting the importance of the assertion by drawing attention to it, while on the other hand depriving the reader of an exact reference. Thus, the reader responds because of the universality of the appeal, but does so in a state of obscurity. Brilliantly, in these few lines Rhys obliges the reader to make a voyage in the dark. By some trick of irony, the blind spot, or ellipsis, which effects an omission from the text – in this case, of the sex act – creates a gap in the discourse which is filled with an appeal to ultimate knowledge, itself the very opposite of innocence. The fundamental nature of this type of experience is highlighted by the five-fold repetition of 'always' which is used in its delimitation. And the paradoxical question posed at the end of this italicised section throws into debate the whole notion of truth, allowing the dilemma to sound on in the text without any answer. On a less philosophical level too, the use of 'always' works to suggest inevitability. This adds a certain fatalism to the way of seeing which informs the text. The state of innocence is thus circumscribed by a subjection to such necessity, and this sombre thought invites us to share her perception of the world as a tragic place. Perhaps this is part of the limitation of choice imposed by the state of blindness. And yet our own response is ambivalent. We are torn between agreeing on the one hand that she is right, and on the other, resisting her view of the world, feeling that her impression of it is too subjective.

Clearly, as far as the text is concerned, Anna herself responds to this sexual experience, a most significant moment in her life, with a coolness which is quite remarkable considering her initial misgivings. The fact is that the narrative registers very little response on her part, in contrast with Walter's concern for what he takes to be a sad expression. Indeed, the only direct thought which she has on the subject is quite dismissive of its importance: 'I thought that it had been just like the girls said, except that I hadn't known it would hurt so much.' Significantly enough, this assertion is evidence of her reliance on others for advice. But the implication of this comparative reticence is that she has just suffered disillusionment, and the feeling of detachment which it elicits is linked with another important way in which her sense of blindness is suggested in the text, that is, through the use of the mirror.

A survey of the use of the mirror, or 'glass' as Rhys calls it, will demonstrate its importance in the novel not only as a distancing device but also as a means through which Anna's symbolic death may be reflected in the narrative. There is about Anna's mirror-madness an almost Lacanian sense of her own identity as an absence or fiction.[10] The implications of this are disturbing. It is through her response to the sequence of mirrors in the discourse that we gradually see into the epicentre of the work itself, when an idea of nihilism is generated.

We have already observed the first of the references to mirrors which had occurred on Anna's initial meeting with Walter Jeffries. A significant point about this instance is that Anna makes no comment on what she sees: 'I watched myself in the glass over the mantelpiece, laughing.' This laconicism contrasts with Maudie's comment on what she observes when she views herself, a little later in the text: 'She watched herself in the mirror. "I'm getting lines under my eyes, aren't I?"' In this way, Maudie uses the mirror quite naturally to examine her face. This 'normal' use throws Anna's use of the glass into sharp relief, emphasising the effect of detachment which it brings about. By implication, the lack of any textual reference to a reflection suggests an absence of the reflection one might expect to see. Already, this foreshadows the idea of Anna as a ghost, as someone unreal whose image is not reflected in the normal way. Indeed, Anna notes that Walter looks

at her as if she were not there. This occurs when she rejects his
sexual advances:

> "I'm very sorry," he said. "That was extremely stupid of me."
> Looking at me with his eyes narrow and close together, as if he
> hated me, as if I wasn't there; and then he turned away and
> looked at himself in the glass. (p.20)

Obviously, his own response on seeing his appearance is not given
in a text in which the point of view belongs to someone else, and it
is unlikely that he will comment on it in view of what has just
occurred. His very act of looking at himself thus may be due
merely to the immediate dashing of his plans – a natural reaction of
embarrassment, perhaps, in which he turns away from Anna who
has just rejected him.

Anna's behaviour after this incident is important too, and again
involves the mirror. By this time she has moved away from Walter
into the adjoiing room:

> There was a fire but the room was cold. I walked up to the
> looking-glass and put the lights on over it and stared at myself. It
> was as if I were looking at somebody else. I stared at myself for a
> long time. . . . (pp.20–1)

Now, added to the sense of detachment comes a schizoid feeling of
otherness which allows Anna to view herself with an impression of
complete dislocation. In effect, the 'somebody else' present in the
reflection has no connection with the eye perceiving it, and the
omission in the text of any identifying features emphasises both
the alienation of this otherness and the split which allows the
thinking, feeling Anna to operate completely separately from the
bodily presence evident in the glass. This split, then, further
suggests the ghostliness of the body which, thus deprived of any
spirit, is but a dead reflection. And Anna's subsequent awareness
supports this idea: 'I felt as if I had gone out of myself, as if I were
in a dream.' In such a state of dislocation everything seems unreal
to her: 'The fire was like a painted fire; no warmth came from it',
and her own bodily temperature, cold as the dead, contrasts with
the heat which she perceives: 'When I put my hand against my
face it was very cold and my face was hot.'

The idea of others perceiving in Anna a lack of animation and life is extended even to the minor characters, the proprietors of the dress shop with its 'two long mirrors' (p.24). There, 'the thin Miss Cohen' treats her as if she were 'a doll', and Anna's detached 'face in the glass looked small and frightened'. From a textual point of view this is a fascinating admission, for it is made quite implicitly. We are not prepared for it by any indication that Anna has just looked into the glass. Instead, her perception is woven into the text without any qualifying introduction, and the effect is to highlight the impression of detachment. This experience of dislocation extends even to her direct perception of her surroundings when, without viewing them in a mirror, she comments that 'the streets looked different that day, just as a reflection in the looking-glass is different from the real thing.' The very choice of simile demonstrates Anna's mental preoccupation with mirrors, but it also draws attention to the distorting effect achieved through their use. There is irony at work here, for the fact that Anna spends so much of her time gazing into mirrors suggests that her view of life is itself distorted. The effect of this double-edged observation is very like that of the detail about the position of the window in *After Leaving Mr Mackenzie*. In this later novel it is another example of the irony through which the 'narrating I' can modify our impression of the behaviour of the 'narrated I'.

The function of the mirror as a distancing device, and Anna's private obsession with it, are suggested in two important passages in which, rather than using the glass to look at herself, she even uses it to observe Walter:

> He came into the room again and I watched him in the glass. My handbag was on the table. He took it up and put some money into it. Before he did it he looked towards me but he thought I couldn't see him. I got up. I meant to say, "What are you doing?" But when I went up to him instead of saying, "Don't do that," I said. "All right, if you like – anything you like, any way you like." And I kissed his hand. (pp.33–4)

Here, Anna can distance herself from a direct observation of Walter and, therefore, from a complicity in his action of putting money into her purse. The distance gives her time consciously to prepare a response which is different from the one which she actually finds herself making. Walter's action soon becomes an established pattern which will be continued by his successor, Carl Redman. It serves two purposes. Firstly, for him, this payment for sexual favours devalues the emotional significance of the act, suggesting that he sees Anna as a mere commodity. In this respect, a remark which Maudie relates to Anna a little later is shown to have dramatic irony: ' "D'you know what a man said to me the other day? It's funny, he said, have you ever thought that a girl's clothes cost more than the girl inside them?" ' (pp.39–40). We recall that Walter's first gift of £25 was made in order that Anna might buy 'some stockings' (p.23). The amount which he gives her here is undisclosed, and this time no mention is made of its purpose. Secondly, the manner in which Anna accepts the money is worth noting. The gesture of kissing his hand is symbolic of the abject manner which such dependence can lead to. Indeed, this behaviour is accomplished through a subconscious urge – we have already seen that the conscious response which she had prepared would have been quite different. Almost immediately afterwards, Anna herself is embarrassed and confused by it: 'I felt miserable suddenly and utterly lost. "Why did I do that?" I thought.' But it is too late to reverse her action, and the inexorable trail of descent is set in motion. Lest we should miss the significance of this interchange, the narrator leaves us in no doubt as to its meaning when, at the end of the chapter, the taxi driver winks at Anna: 'When I paid the man he winked at me. I looked over his head and pretended not to notice.' On this occasion her pretence is accomplished in a less subtle fashion than that afforded by the presence of the mirror which had allowed her to observe without seeming to do so.

On the second occasion when Anna observes Walter in the mirror, her use of the glass is a much more sustained and open one. It occurs during a week-end spent away with him, in the aftermath of a disagreement between his cousin Vincent and Germaine. After Germaine's angry departure from the room, Anna, in order to avoid any more of the unpleasantness, leaves the two men to discuss the dispute alone, on the pretext of going to the lavatory. Eventually, Walter joins her after an ellipsis which ends on Anna in her bedroom in what has become her characteristic place, positioned in front of the mirror: 'I was standing in front of the long glass in the bedroom when Walter came in.' (p.71). The use of the imperfect tense here gives no indication of the length of time which she had already occupied in this way, and there is no reference to any reason for her presence there. Indeed, throughout the subsequent interchange with Walter, apart from one short break when she necessarily moves away in order to begin to pack her suitcase, Anna remains fixed before the glass, obliging him to communicate with a reflection rather than with her actual face. It is suggested, not directly stated, that this physical position is maintained, by a repeated reference to it a little later in the diegesis when Walter has just announced that one of the reasons for the disagreement is that Vincent is going away for a while. This provides him with an opportunity to introduce the subject of his own departure:

> "Oh, is he going away?" I said. I was still looking in the glass.
> He said, "Yes, I'm going to New York next week and I'm taking him with me."
> I didn't say anything. I put my face nearer the glass. Like when you're a kid and you put your face very near to the glass and make faces at yourself. (p.72)

Clearly, the mirror acts here as a barrier between the two of them, and it is likely that Walter himself also appreciates its distancing function in this instance. Perhaps he finds it easier to broach bad news before a reflection than before flesh and blood. Anna's own response on hearing what he has to say is to move nearer to the glass, and by doing so she draws the image of herself closer to her own body and therefore away from his sight. This is a symbolic gesture which allows her to remove herself from him and at the same time to cover up any possible facial register of response, leaving only her back in view. The simile of the child making grimaces further deflects and explains away any signs of change in her own features, but it also momentarily puts her in the role of the rebellious minor whose only means of showing contempt is by sticking out her tongue in the face of authority.

After this occasion of Anna effectively blocking Walter's access to her reflection by interposing her bodily self between them, there is a reduced use of the mirror in the text, and, indeed, a reversion to its 'normal' function. In its place, Anna's attention, the direction of her focus, falls onto an area which is both imaginative and quite macabre. Instead of the disturbing absence of a reflection, which had implicitly suggested the idea of Anna as a ghost, there is now a much more explicit suggestion of her in an attitude of death.

The first of these moments, and the most vivid, occurs during Anna's final meeting with Walter, in the course of which she tries to come to terms with his rejection of her. Prior to their discussion, the idea of death is introduced when, mentally, she anticipates her plea to him:

> I imagined myself saying, very calmly, "The thing is that you don't understand. You think I want more than I do. I only want to see you sometimes, but if I never see you again I'll die. I'm dying now really, and I'm too young to die." (p.83)

Her distracted state of mind is reflected not only in the abject quality of this projected utterance, but also in the subsequent flashback to a moment in the past when she had attended a funeral:

> ... The candles crying wax tears and the smell of stephanotis and I had to go to the funeral in a white dress and white gloves and a wreath round my head and the wreath in my hands made my gloves wet – they said so young to die ...
> The people there were like upholstered ghosts.

There is something deeply ironic in the image of the 'wax tears'. Firstly, it does give an insight into the imaginative perception of the young child who experiences the funeral. But the hand of the 'narrating I' may be seen at work in the subtlety of the suggestion of false grief which the idea of 'wax' adds to the image of the tears. This is reminiscent of Flaubert's embroidered tears in the decoration on the pall covering Madame Bovary's coffin: 'Le drap noir, semé de larmes blanches, se levait de temps à autre en découvrant la bière.'[11] Unlike the Flaubertian example, however, the texture of the irony in the Rhys passage draws less attention to itself. The use of the present participle is important in this respect, for it suggests an impressionistic rendering and an immediacy which deflects the focus away from the significance of the image, placing it rather on the intensity of the flashback which is highlighted by this sudden alteration in tense. Nevertheless, the sheer imagination which this passage displays is underlined in the remarkable image of the 'upholstered ghosts' with which the moment ends. This opens up a disturbing idea of the living dead. Those funeral guests who, in their best clothes, resemble stuffed and decorated spectres, pre-

pare us for the notion of Anna's own spiritual demise, an emotional decease which will imply the waxing over of her tears. Furthermore, the ambiguity which arises through the fact that the
subject of this particular funeral is not distinguished, has an
important part to play in the evocation of this idea of Anna's own
death. The heavy symbolism of the white, foregrounded here in its
repetition – a colour not only associated with the pallor of death
itself but also with the shroud – couples with that of the 'wreath',
also repeated, to load Anna's own appearance with significance.
But perhaps most suggestive of all is the syntax of the whole
passage, which aligns the repeated phrase 'young to die' with the
subject of the paragraph – here again, as in the previous one –
Anna herself. The importance of this suggestive use of language is
seen in its transformation of an apparently simple flashback into a
symbolic anticipation of Anna's own funeral.

With the idea of death thus firmly established in the reader's
mind, the discourse moves on towards the first of those more
explicit references. Walter's rejection of Anna's suggestion that
they return to his house rather than discuss their affair in a public
place is the stimulus for a most macabre imaginative moment:

> He said, "Why do you ask me the one thing you know
> perfectly well I won't do?"
> I didn't answer. I was thinking, "You don't know anything
> about me. I don't care any more." And I didn't care any more.
> It was like letting go and falling back into water and seeing
> yourself grinning up through the water, your face like a mask,
> and seeing the bubbles coming up as if you were trying to speak
> from under the water. And how do you know what it's like to try
> to speak from under water when you're drowned? "And I've
> met a lot of them who were monkeys too," he said . . . (p.84)

The abandonment of the looking-glass as a distancing device leads
to a liberation of the imagination. This is appreciated most in such
a passage as that above, in which the narrator finds other means of
suggesting her own sense of alienation. Here, instead of focusing
on a reflection of herself, disembodiment is achieved through a
much more disturbing effect of depersonalisation, in which the
focus falls on a mental image of the subject herself, unmediated by
any mirror. Thus, the resulting sense of distance between the
perceiving mind and the object of perception, arises from within

that mind itself, with a disquieting suggestion of a schizoid mentality. The suggestion of drowning is rendered macabre through the image of the face 'grinning up through the water', and the simile of the 'mask' encapsulates the idea both of the death mask, and the rigidity of the facial characteristics made strange through rigor mortis. This idea of death conflicts with that of the attempt to speak, thus adding to the defamiliarisation which the whole concept undergoes in this passage. And the apparently random utterance on the subject of 'monkeys' adds a touch of the grotesque to this effect. The utterance is not a random one at all, it is a recapitulation by Anna of certain words her father once spoke in response to the ridiculing of a French governor of their island home.[12] Their repetition here is symptomatic of Anna's disturbed state of mind at this point. But they also echo an earlier textual analepsis, another of Anna's memories, and by doing so, end what may be taken to be an imaginative prolepsis on a retrospective note, thus treating the temporal status of the novel with an anarchic disregard.

Although the passage is not formally presented in the style of a prolepsis, clearly, as far as the diegesis is concerned, the idea of Anna's death relates to a future occurrence. This is understood in the narrative rhetoric: '. . . how do you know what it's like . . . ?' But the actual use of this anticipated moment as a means of comparison in a simile alters the normal level of a prolepsis by giving it the status of experience already undergone. This is a most complex technical achievement which highlights the potential for variation in the temporal duality of the narrative, that is, in the way in which the actual time of the diegesis relates to the narrative time of the discourse. Just as this technical freedom allowed the death of Fifi to occur in the narrative itself prior to her actual death in the course of the diegesis, so, here too, Anna's death can take place in the discourse before her actual death is achieved. This, indeed, appears to be the aim of such a subversive use of technique in this novel.

The idea of death by drowning is continued implicitly a little later, in the narrator's imaginative use of metaphor which could suggest the swelling of Anna's body brought about by an absorption of water: 'I stretched, and watched my swollen shadow on the wall stretching too.' (p.96). Again, the redundant mirror is replaced by a new distancing device, that of the shadow reflected onto a wall. This idea is employed again at a moment when Anna feels

excluded from the fun and laughter which her friends, Laurie and
Joe, enjoy. This time, the shadows reflected belong to the others,
and Anna's perception of them implies a reduction of their stature
which is stimulated by her own sense of alienation from them:
'They were sitting near the fire laughing. Their black shadows on
the wall were laughing too.' (p.106). Such a depersonalisation of
her so-called friends into mere shades emphasises the difficulty
which Anna experiences in relating to people. It echoes the idea of
others as 'upholstered ghosts', as incorporeal beings with whom
any real communication is impossible. And the use of 'black' in the
image, symbolic both of impurity and evil, adds to the idea of a
contrast with that whiteness which we now associate with Anna.

Anna's tendency to depersonalise, however, is seen not only in
her transference of focus onto other people's shadows, but is even
exercised in her perception of their physical beings. This is how,
through the use of close-up detail, the human aspect of Laurie's
facial characteristics is rendered unrecognisable. Here, alcohol
plays an important part in stimulating the distortion, but the
significance of this particular moment in Anna's perceptive life
may not, therefore, be dismissed. Rather, the fact that drink
gradually becomes a feature of her life implies that this sort of
perception will occur with increasing regularity. In this passage,
Anna focuses on Laurie's face as the older girl helps her to take off
the dress which she had lent her:

> She came over and helped me to undo it. She seemed very tall
> and her face enormous. I could see all the lines in it, and the
> powder, trying to fill up the lines, and just where her lipstick
> stopped and her lips began. It looked like a clown's face, so that I
> wanted to laugh at it. She was pretty but her hands were short
> and fat with wide, flat, very red nails. (p.106)

The effect of depersonalisation through a detailed focus on certain
features, in a style which anticipates that of Alain Robbe-Grillet,
perhaps, distorts with an almost surrealistic effect.

Earlier, I suggested that Anna's sensibility was exceptional.
Certainly, her withdrawal into the imaginative recesses of her
mind, which these passages bear witness to, would seem to lend
weight to that assertion. Not everyone, whether assisted through
alcohol or not, would perceive the world in this way. Rhys ensures
that attention is drawn to Anna's difference of aspect by incorpo-

rating into the text certain comments of her friends about her personality. Laurie plays an important part in this respect. At the end of the night out with Joe, she sums up her feelings about Anna's behaviour:

> "What you do doesn't concern me," Laurie said. "I think you're a bit of a fool, that's all. And I think you'll never get on, because you don't know how to take people. After all, to say you'll come out with somebody and then to get tight and start a row about nothing at all isn't a way to behave. And besides, you always look half-asleep and people don't like that. But it's not my business." (p.110)

The movement from her particular grievance, specific to the evening which they have just spent together, to a more general criticism, is instructive. The assertion that Anna always looks 'half-asleep' focuses on her essential difference from others. It points to some characteristic at a source which is deep within her psyche, and possibly refers to that idiosyncratic withdrawal from the world incurred by her reliance upon the imaginative faculty.

A little later in the discourse, Ethel Matthews reinforces the idea of Anna's difference when she, too, criticises the younger woman for not living up to her expectations, that is, for not making the most of her potential as a woman to use men:

> "I wanted a smart girl," she said, "who'd be a bit nice to people and the way you seemed I thought you were the sort of kid who'd take the trouble to be nice to people and make a few friends and so on and try to make the place go. And as a matter of fact you're enough to drive anybody crazy with that potty look of yours." (p.124)

Clearly, the 'potty look' ties in with Laurie's observations of Anna being 'half-asleep'. The derogatory tone implied by the phrase, however, sums up the intolerance of other people when faced with individuality. In choosing Anna to assist her in the business, Ethel Matthews could not have picked a worse candidate to mould into the required shape. Besides her habit of mental distraction, Anna's natural resistance to conformity, as well as her disinclination to kowtow to others, makes her a poor prospect for the world of service.

Ethel's attempt to exploit Anna is doomed from the start, therefore, and it results in an explosive situation in which Anna rejects the older woman's values in a symbolic act of mindless destruction. This is an important incident, for the symbolism involved is connected with a network of images of 'glass' which not only develop from the concept of the 'looking-glass' but also continue the function in the novel originally performed by it. Thus, the newly formed concept of 'glass' serves a similar purpose to that of Anna's contemplation of shadows rather than reflections. I will return to a discussion of the climactic incident in which Anna destroys a picture belonging to Ethel, a little later. For the moment, I wish to clarify the idea of this new structure by focusing on its gradual development within the text.

So accustomed do we become to the concept of the mirror being designated by the signifier 'glass', that the first alternative use of the same signifier may cause a momentary check in our understanding. It occurs quite late in the novel, near the beginning of Part Three, when Anna, having moved into Ethel's flat in Bird Street, accepts an invitation to go out with Laurie and two men whom she has just picked up. The actual outing in the diegesis is reduced in the text into a mere sixteen lines, of which only three correspond to any dialogue which occurred, the remainder being concerned with the movement of Anna's consciousness during the excursion. This very textual approach itself signifies the extent to which Anna has withdrawn into the recesses of her own imagination:

> It was one of those days when you can see the ghosts of all the other lovely days. You drink a bit and watch the ghosts of all the lovely days that have ever been from behind a glass. (p.122)

The metaphorical application of the term 'glass' in this use of it partly accounts for any initial ambiguity of meaning. To look at something through a glass implies that a difference of perception will be caused by the effect of the alcohol which had originally been in the glass. Clearly, this is what the narrator intends to suggest. However, the subtle alteration of the preposition 'through' to 'from behind' complicates the issue. Whereas it is quite possible to situate oneself 'behind' a looking-glass, or even a sheet of glass, as in a window, it is an odd term to use in relation to a drinking glass. And the effect of one's vision penetrating this 'glass' suggests, moreover, that it is a clear sheet of glass rather than a mirror, for it is impossible to see through the latter unless it has a two-way effect. Consequently, I would suggest that it is through such ambiguity that attention is drawn to the alteration of meaning implied by the new use of the signifier 'glass'. A further complication arises, however, in the floating significance of this word. Up until this moment in the text the meaning of the term has been fixed – 'glass' has signified 'mirror'. Now, though, each subsequent use of the term implies a different concept. Take, for instance, another metaphorical use of the word when it is employed to convey the effect of the clarity and smoothness of the sea, in a dream which Anna relates:

> I dreamt that I was on a ship. From the deck you could see small islands – dolls of islands – and the ship was sailing in a doll's sea, transparent as glass. (p.140)

Clearly, the glass here relates to that of any window pane, with the transparency of which a comparison may be drawn to the lucidity of the sea. There is nothing unusual about this particular metaphorical application. What is significant, however, is the characteristic of transparency which is a common feature of all the new uses of the term. Now, instead of the 'glass' throwing back a reflection, the function is altered so that there is no potential for an image of the perceiver to be shown when she uses it. In effect, then, the novelist has achieved a new deployment of the concept so that the lack of a reflection, which has so far been suggested textually, actually becomes part and parcel of the design. In this respect, if we were to examine the concept anew, from the point in the text where 'glass' signifies a material with translucent qualities, we would see that the characteristic of non-reflection now actually inheres in the concept itself, where earlier that characteristic had been anticipated laterally through textual suggestion. Thus, as the novel develops, so there is a clarification of meaning which adds to the sense of inexorability about the *progression d'effet*.[13]

Also adding to the *progression d'effet* is that build-up of tension in Anna which leads to her increased withdrawal from the society of other people, and to a greater introspection. Ethel Matthews plays a significant part in this movement of Anna's consciousness, although she cannot be blamed for what is, at base, a natural inclination in the younger girl. However, her overbearing attitude,

financial exploitation, and neurotic behaviour do seem to acceler-
ate the development of this tendency, and partly explain Anna's
act of destruction which I referred to earlier.

The incident occurs at the end of an evening which Anna has
spent with a man whom she has casually picked up. This situation
in itself, coupled with the fact that throughout the passage the man
is never referred to by name, is a sign of Anna's moral decline. A
most enlightening paragraph in this respect, is that in which there
is a brief physical description of him:

> He had a little, close-clipped moustache and one wrist was
> bandaged. Why was it bandaged? I don't know, I didn't ask. He
> didn't look as nice as I had thought when he spoke to me. I had
> gone by his voice. His eyes were a bit bleary. (p.137)

The remarkable indifference to him which Anna displays in this
extract is a by-product both of her loss of innocence and her
increased introspection. By this time, quite late in the text, she has
ceased to have any interest in developing personal relationships
with the men she meets. The eventual breakdown of communication between herself and Ethel Matthews may, to a certain extent,
be seen to be a corollary of this indifference. In the sense that
Anna's disillusionment with men arises from her recognition that
they exploit women, her rejection of Matthews arises from her
gradual perception of the latter's motives. As yet, Anna's response
to Ethel may not be said to be indifferent – such a feeling will come
later;[14] on the contrary, the act of violence which she perpetrates
against the older woman's possessions is a positive assertion of her
contempt for the way in which she has been used:

> "What's this one? *Connais-tu le pays?* Do you know the country
> where the orange-tree flowers? Let's try that."
> "No, it gives me the pip," I said.
> I put on *Just a Little Love, a Little Kiss* and then *Puppchen* again.
> We started to dance and while we were dancing the dog in the
> picture over the bed stared down at us smugly. (Do you know
> the country? Of course, if you know the country it makes all the
> difference. The country where the orange-tree flowers?)
> I said, "I can't stand that damned dog any longer."
> I stopped dancing and took off my shoe and threw it at the
> picture. The glass smashed.

"I've wanted to do that for weeks," I said.

He said, "Good shot. But we're making rather a row, aren't we?"

I said, "It's all right. We can make as much noise as we like. It doesn't matter. I should bloody well like to see her come up and say anything if I bloody well want to make a row."

"Oh, quite," he said, looking at me sideways. (pp.137–8)

Throughout the text, in any description of Ethel's flat, attention has been drawn to the stereotyped character of the decoration.[15] Undoubtedly, 'the picture of the dog sitting up begging – *Loyal Heart*' (p.127), fits into this category of signs. In the passage quoted above, an implicit contrast is provided to the uniformity which such stereotyping implies; this is found in the content of Goethe's song which Anna refuses to hear: 'Connais-tu le pays?' Here, Rhys adapts the song to her own purpose, subordinating the original context – the German longing for Italy – and implying that it signifies Anna's longing for her Caribbean home. Anna's assertion that it 'gives me the pip' is, of course, an excuse to avoid the emotion which personal memories of 'the country where the orange-tree flowers' – her island home – would elicit in her. By now, of course, we recognise that any positive natural imagery in the text is associated with her youth in Dominica, the days of her innocence and comparative happiness. Consequently, its intrusion into her present environment – the bedroom of a massage parlour – adds a certain irony to her situation. No doubt, a subconscious recognition that she will never be able to return to that innocent past accounts for the sudden violent attack on what may be seen to be a symbol of her own abasement. But the fact that the picture of the dog belongs to Ethel may explain Anna's dramatic response on her recognition of smugness in its features. Clearly, this is a human characteristic which she probably associates with Ethel, and so her reaction to the picture may be taken to be an expression of her feelings towards Matthews herself.

A most significant feature of the description of this incident, however, may be seen in the lean account of the damage caused, and the lack of ensuing emotion expressed in the text. The economy with which the narrator states that 'The glass smashed' is quite striking, and when this is coupled with Anna's words: 'I've wanted to do that for weeks' it seems to point to some extra significance. The fact that it is the 'glass' which is damaged, and that, as far as we know, the picture itself remains unharmed,[16] suggests that her words apply to the actual shattering of the glass. This action has given her some satisfaction, and it would not be surprising to learn that it was the destruction of the glass which had been intended, even if only subconsciously. The text itself maintains a silence on this point by avoiding any narrative comment on Anna's response to her uncharacteristic act of destruction. This is quite unusual, for one might at least have expected a brief comment on the altered appearance of the dog which had appeared to stimulate the incident. Such a textual silence would seem to lend weight to the idea that the picture itself was not, after all, the genuine goal of the damage. Indeed, the fact that this is the very first time that Anna has expressed any negative feelings about the picture is further evidence to support this view.

Given that Anna's earlier preoccupation with the 'glass' became obsessive, it is quite conceivable that the smashing of the 'glass' here relates to it in some way. Indeed, every use of the term 'glass' in the novel must ultimately be associated, through a homonymous relationship alone, if for no other reason. Could this action, therefore, be a gesture symbolic of the destruction of the mirror? Certainly, Anna has no further use for the looking-glass; indeed, the one remaining reference to it subsequent to this incident may offer a possible explanation for such redundancy. This final direct reference to the mirror is connected to the drama just analysed, by virtue of the fact that it is contained within the same chapter, but it occurs on a different narrative level owing to its position in a flashback to childhood days in Dominica:

> Obeah zombis soucriants – lying in the dark frightened of the dark frightened of soucriants that fly in through the window and suck your blood – they fan you to sleep with their wings and then they suck your blood – you know them in the day-time – they look like people but their eyes are red and staring and they're soucriants at night – looking in the glass and thinking sometimes my eyes look like a soucriant's eyes . . . (pp.139–40)

This passage is most important, for it brings to a climax a structure which has been fundamental to the development of the novel – the use of the term 'glass' to signify 'mirror'. Throughout the novel there has been a constant suggestion of doubt about the living reality of Anna. This has been observed in her own obsession with death, and textually too, in the lack of a reference in the discourse to any reflection of herself thrown back by the mirror. Now, the theme of death is opened out vividly in this flashback to a moment of imagination in childhood. By some textual paradox, this means of reaching back into the past to evoke a memory which, thanks to the use of the present tense, is rendered in the discourse as freshly as it was originally experienced, actually accomplishes a forward movement – it puts into perspective those obsessions in Anna's character which have perplexed us throughout the course of the work. The intensity of this outline of her fascination with the island voodoo, and her imaginative involvement in that world, must account, in part, for that development of her sense of alienation from other people. Certainly, this is proof of the exceptional sensitivity of her mind which had marked her out as different from them. So powerful is the imagination displayed here that the effect of this childhood dream remains with her throughout her life and affects all of her adult relationships.

The first-person narrative mode used in *Voyage in the Dark* brought with it a need to look into the substance of the one voice itself in order to determine the complexity of the personality. In Anna's narrative, I have observed a developing network of structures which has had a serious contribution to make to our understanding of her sense of alienation from the society in which she lives. I should now like to examine Sasha Jansen's first-person narrative voice in *Good Morning, Midnight*, in which a distinct bifurcation makes for a sense of self-mockery which was completely lacking in Anna's view of herself, and which engenders a wholly individual flavour, a wholly individual 'Rhys woman'.

5

Sasha in Narrative Control

The second autodiegetic[1] novel in the Rhys canon – *Good Morning, Midnight* – differs from its predecessor most particularly in the sense that, throughout the text, the impression is created that Sasha is in firm control of her own narrative, and that the picture which she presents of herself to the implied reader is one which has been carefully striven for. To a great extent, Sasha's own self-irony accounts for this impression. We see it arise through a distinct bifurcation of her voice into two parts, which allows her, at times, to engage in a mental dialogue with herself. She puts this divided voice both to comic and serious use, and in the course of this chapter I shall examine it closely as it operates in each of these dimensions. But we also see her exercise great control over the emotional content of her discourse, careful always to recount the most painful episodes in her life with a detachment which actually manages to augment the sense of suffering. An analysis of the means by which she achieves this will form another substantial part of this chapter.

The split in the narrative voice comes into effect very early in the novel. Often, it allows a conversation to occur within Sasha's mind. At such times, the use of 'you' functions as a mental construct to enable the discussion between the two parts of the voice. This movement may be observed in three important paragraphs in the first chapter:

> Never mind, I have some money now. I may be able to do something about it. Twelve o'clock on a fine autumn day, and nothing to worry about. Some money to spend and nothing to worry about.
> But careful, careful! Don't get excited. You know what happens when you get excited and exalted, don't you? ... Yes. ... And then, you know how you collapse like a pricked balloon, don't you? Having no staying power. ... Yes, exactly. ... So, no excitement. This is going to be a quiet, sane fortnight. Not too

much drinking, avoidance of certain cafés, of certain streets, of certain spots, and everything will go off beautifully.

The thing is to have a programme, not to leave anything to chance – no gaps. No trailing around aimlessly with cheap gramophone records starting up in your head, no "Here this happened, here that happened." Above all, no crying in public, no crying at all if you can help it. (p.14)

The alteration from the use of the personal pronoun in the first of the above paragraphs to the second-person pronoun in the second and third, marks the difference in tone. As yet, the alternative voice provides some gentle self-mockery, but gradually, as the novel continues, a much more severely ironic tone will become established. Then the criticism will have a broader reach, extending, at times, to society in general, and not always being confined to Sasha's own personal circumstances. For the moment, however, the voice concerns itself with Sasha's potentially embarrassing behaviour during what promises to be a very nostalgic fortnight for her. A certain piquancy is achieved at this outset when the time-limit of two weeks, of which she is so conscious, is implicitly set against the enormous amount of experience which she had previously undergone in this city. Somehow, the 'quiet, sane fortnight' which she forecasts for herself seems to be doomed from the start when seen against her obsessive fear of 'crying in public' over the memories elicited by her old haunts.

As I have already suggested, the split in the narrative voice serves to evoke a sense of self-irony in Sasha. An examination of the remembered scene in which Mr Blank, the English director of the dress shop where she used to work, pays one of his quarterly visits to the staff in Paris, will demonstrate the bifurcation of the voice, not only showing it to add to the comic effect of the episode, but also demonstrating Sasha's ability to laugh at herself. It is this quality which makes her personality so unique in the respect of the 'Rhys woman'. Neither Marya, nor Julia, nor Anna were able to mock themselves to this degree.

The text moves directly into a dramatic rendering of the scene, employing the present tense to increase the drama of the passage and add to the comic effect which is engineered by the narrative handling of the discourse. The initial paragraph in the present tense sets the tone for the whole of the 'Mr Blank' sequence:

> He arrives. Bowler-hat, majestic trousers, oh-my-God express-
> ion, ha-ha eyes – I know him at once. He comes up the steps
> with Salvatini behind him, looking very worried. (Salvatini is the
> boss of our shop.) Don't let him notice me, don't let him look at
> me. Isn't there something you can do so that nobody looks at
> you or sees you? Of course, you must make your mind vacant,
> neutral – you are invisible.
> No use. He comes up to my table. (p.17)

The humour is immediately unleashed in the description of him,
which manages to suggest a stereotype while retaining freshness
and originality in the imagery used. The audacity of the epithet
'majestic' as applied to 'trousers' is most apposite, as well as comic
in such a combination. Salvatini's timid role in the affair, by
contrasting with the overbearing disdain of this man, assists in
inflating his air of superiority still further. Sasha's own nervousness is not ameliorated thereby. Having said that, however, there is
a moment in this paragraph which seems to suggest that her fear is
carefully striven for rather than genuinely felt. I do not mean to
suggest that the writing is insincere, but rather that the narrator is
enjoying a game with her narrative by sending herself up for the
sheer delight of the reader. This moment occurs with the bracketed
utterance, by which the narrator signifies that her discourse is
directed to an implied reader – '(Salvatini is the boss of our shop.)'
Of course, the whole status of the narrative is altered at this point.
The situation is a most complex one. The present tense is employed to create the illusion that the action is happening at the time
it is apprehended by the reader. No mediating phrase of the type 'I
can see myself . . .'[2] qualifies this use of the present. Consequently,
the appearance of this bracketed information, information which is
directed specifically to the implied reader, breaks into the linear
contiguity of the text and therefore disrupts the illusion. It suggests
that the narrator is very much aware of her audience, and because
of this, it is now possible to view the tenor of Sasha's paranoia with
some scepticism. On a closer examination, the descriptive terms
which she has coined in her portrait of the man may be seen to tell
us nothing whatsoever about him. In fact, each one, apart from the
detail of the 'bowler-hat', is peculiarly non-visual; what, for instance are 'ha-ha eyes'? And yet, on a first reading we responded
to this picture much as she directed us to do. Such is the power of
the narrative. Perhaps even more disturbing, though, is her

present attitude to what is an important and serious theme running through the novel – that of the question of Sasha's lack of a sense of identity. Certainly, her fear asserts itself in the form of a desire to become 'vacant, neutral' and 'invisible'. The humorous anticlimax achieved in the text by the words 'No use. . . .' punctures the earnestness of the desire to disappear, rendering the emotions comic. Again, therefore, the narrator may be shown to be sending herself up.

Undoubtedly, the use of Sasha's second voice is invaluable in adding to the versatility of the tone established in the novel as a whole. Within the 'Mr Blank' sequence, the voice is characterised by an address to 'my dear sir' rather than to the second-person pronoun which we have already seen in operation elsewhere. This characteristic may be best observed in a passage of internalised conversation which occurs while Sasha is being questioned on the subject of her knowledge of foreign languages:

> Of course, sometimes, when I am a bit drunk and am talking to somebody I like and know, I speak French very fluently indeed. At other times I just speak it. And as to that, my dear sir, you've got everything all wrong. I'm here because I have a friend who knows Mr Salvatini's mistress, and Mr Salvatini's mistress spoke to Mr Salvatini about me, and the day that he saw me I wasn't looking too bad and he was in a good mood. Nothing at all to do with fluent French and German, dear sir, nothing at all. I'm here because I'm here because I'm here. And just to prove to you that I speak French, I'll sing you a little song about it: Si vous saviez, si vous saviez, si vous saviez comment ça se fait.
>
> For God's sake, I think, pull yourself together.
>
> I say: "I speak French fairly well. I've been living in Paris for eight years." (p.18)

The exhortation to 'pull yourself together' demonstrates that the tone adopted in the preceding paragraph is in character for her address to herself, but is not part of her public persona. This suggestion adds to our impression that her second voice is, indeed, not her natural one, and that she feels uncomfortable, possibly even mentally dispossessed, on the occasions when it takes over from her natural diffidence. It is used here for comic effect, the actual utterance which Sasha does manage to convey being far more timid than that which the second voice would have given had it been permitted to find breath.

The effort to effect a send-up of the narrator herself is most clearly revealed in a further exchange between Sasha and the director:

> Salvatini puts his head out of the door behind me and says: "Mr Blank wants to see you."
>
> I at once make up my mind that he wants to find out if I can speak German. All the little German I know flies out of my head. Jesus, Help me! Ja, ja, nein, nein, was kostet es, Wien ist eine sehr schöne Stadt, Buda-Pest auch ist sehr schöne, ist schöne, mein Herr, ich habe meinen Blumen vergessen, aus meinen grossen Schmerzen, homo homini lupus, aus meinen grossen Schmerzen mach ich die kleinen Lieder, homo homini lupus (I've got that one, anyway), aus meinen grossen Schmerzen homo homini doh ré mi fah soh la ti doh. . . .
>
> He is sitting at the desk, writing a letter. I stand there. He is sure to notice how shabby my shoes are.
>
> Salvatini looks up, gives me a furtive smile and then looks away again. (p.21)

The use of the name 'Blank' to signify the London boss sets the artificial tone of the entire passage. It is heavy with irony. It suggests that this character's importance is negligible, and consequently, the panic of Sasha's neurotic response to him is highlighted. The present participle used to suggest the calm and lack of concern demonstrated by Mr Blank during this overworking of anxiety on Sasha's part, adds to the comedy of the situation, while Salvatini's cameo role develops the touch of humorous stereotyping which we noticed him provide earlier. During this confrontation, the bifurcation of Sasha's voice is put to comic effect:

> Come on, stand straight, keep your head up, smile. . . . No, don't smile. If you smile he'll think you're trying to get off with him. I know this type. He won't give me the benefit of a shadow of a doubt. Don't smile then, but look eager, alert, attentive. . . . Run out of the door and get away. . . . You fool, stand straight, look eager, alert, attentive. . . . No, look here, he's doing this on purpose. . . . Of course he isn't doing it on purpose. He's just writing a letter. . . . He is, he is. He's doing it on purpose. I know

it, I feel it. I've been standing here for five minutes. This is impossible. (pp.21–2)

Within this paragraph, for the first time in the novel, the narrator brings together in a developed interchange both parts of the split. The result is quite antiphonal, with a voice of reason initiating the series, only to be answered by a voice of dissent. Curiously enough, it is the latter, the voice of dissent, which is this time characterised through being diffident and timid, urging the protagonist to 'run . . . and get away.' And yet, it is this voice which finally induces Sasha to confront her boss with a question:

> "Did you wish to see me, Mr Blank?"
> He looks up and says sharply: "Yes, yes, what is it? What do you want? Wait a minute, wait a minute."
> At once I know. He doesn't want me to talk German, he's going to give me the sack. All right, then, hurry up, get it over. . . .
> Nothing. I just stand there. Now panic has come on me. My hands are shaking, my heart is thumping, my hands are cold. Fly, fly, run from these atrocious voices, these abominable eyes. . . .
> He finishes his letter, writes a line or two on another piece of paper and puts it into an envelope.
> "Will you please take this to the kise?"
> Take this to the kise. . . . I look at Salvatini. He smiles encouragingly.
> Mr Blank rattles out: "Be as quick as you can, Mrs – er – please. Thank you very much."
> I turn and walk blindly through a door. It is a lavatory. They look sarcastic as they watch me going out by the right door. (p.22)

The extravagance of the descriptive terms and the Biblical tone suggested by the lines which urge Sasha to 'Fly . . .', are quite deliberate, creating a parody of the melodrama which informs the whole passage. Mr Blank's failure even to learn Sasha's name gives the lie to her conviction that she is important enough in his eyes to warrant dismissal. But his stumble over her surname is also significant, for it must add to her sense of a lack of personal identity. At the end of the above extract, the comedy becomes effected through the action when Sasha mistakes the lavatory door for the door leading out of the office.

A large part of the humour in this sequence depends for its effect upon a breakdown in communication and a difficulty of interpretation. Sasha's inability to read Mr Blank correctly leads to her feelings of paranoia. Farce is achieved through her lack of recognition of the required door. Most of all, however, the comedy continues for a few more pages owing to her lack of comprehension of Mr Blank's appalling French pronunciation. Clearly, were she a less timorous person, many of these difficulties could be avoided. However, the narrative aim in these pages is a send-up of her own character, and the diffidence of it is played upon for this purpose. But the comic relief has an important part to play in a wider context. There is a seriousness which underlies all of Rhys's humour, and which is brought to the surface most particularly in a passage in which the second voice emerges as the voice of social criticism. Again, the confrontation is between Sasha and the director, although by now the former has overcome her nervousness and is 'no longer afraid of Mr Blank' (p.25):

He looks at me with distaste. Plat du jour – boiled eyes, served cold. . . .

Well, let's argue this out, Mr Blank. You, who represent Society, have the right to pay me four hundred francs a month. That's my market value, for I am an inefficient member of Society, slow in the uptake, uncertain, slightly damaged in the fray, there's no denying it. So you have the right to pay me four hundred francs a month, to lodge me in a small, dark room, to clothe me shabbily, to harrass me with worry and monotony and unsatisfied longings till you get me to the point when I blush at a look, cry at a word. We can't all be happy, we can't all be rich, we can't all be lucky – and it would be so much less fun if we were. Isn't it so, Mr Blank? There must be the dark background to show up the bright colours. Some must cry so that the others may cry so that the others may be able to laugh the more heartily. Sacrifices are necessary. . . . Let's say that you have this mystical right to cut my legs off. But the right to ridicule me afterwards because I am a cripple – no, that I think you haven't got. And that's the right you hold most dearly, isn't it? You must be able to despise the people you exploit. But I wish you a lot of trouble, Mr Blank, and just to start off with, your damned shop's going bust. Alleluia! Did I say all this? Of course I didn't. I didn't even think it. (pp.25–6)

That the narrator takes the man's look of disdain and makes a surrealistic joke of it is important for its effect in mediating the tone of the social criticism which his attitude initiates in the long paragraph to follow. There is a very real danger of the author falling into sermonising when adopting such a critical stance, and technical steps must be taken to ensure that this does not happen. The approach which Rhys adopts seeks to deflate any tendency to sound pompous, by framing the whole message within a tone which is characteristically tongue-in-cheek. Thus, at the beginning of the piece we are directed to envisage a macabre dish-of-the-day, consisting of 'boiled eyes, served cold', while at the end of the piece a devil-may-care attitude takes over, with the director becoming the unconscious butt of the narrator's scorn. But care to keep the criticism within the bounds of acceptability and effectiveness may also be seen in the construction of the paragraph itself. In these lines, the director ceases to be a person, and becomes an anonymous mental construct. This is the point of the label 'Blank'. Through these means, Sasha is able to widen the scope of her criticism, including in it not merely the boss of the particular shop where she works, but every member of the social group which he is seen to 'represent'. But the depersonalisation extends to the narrator too, who momentarily portrays herself not as an individual but as 'an inefficient member of Society', and it is here that the message appears to become so effective. Unlike the mental construct 'Mr Blank', whose character in the novel is always reduced, Sasha's personality quivers before us on every page. Our indignation that the nameless, faceless body which wields the social power should reduce her to a defective cog in the wheel of commerce, is aroused precisely because our sympathies have lain with her from the beginning of the novel. We have responded to her almost as we would do to a genuine human being. And yet, on reflection, we may feel inclined to ask whether there is something cheap about the manner in which our indignation is appealed to. Surely, in view of the cardboard quality of Mr Blank, Rhys cannot seriously expect us to respond thus? Our suspicion of deliberate treachery in the narrative is fuelled by yet another address to the implied reader, which is to be found at the end of the extract: 'Did I say all this? Of course I didn't. I didn't even think it.' And so, the narrative game continues with this qualification which subverts the entire sense of the preceding paragraph. In these three brief sentences the narrator takes the trouble once more to remind the reader of the fabrication of her text, and we are left wondering how to respond in the face of such an audacious disclaimer.

The control which Sasha maintains over her narrative is used not only to render comic certain painful episodes, such as that with Mr Blank, but even, at times, to re-evoke the pain of an experience in as unemotional a way as possible. An examination of a couple of passages, firstly that in which she recounts the death of her baby, will bring out the power of the narrative in this respect:

> The next day she comes in and says: "Now I am going to arrange that you will be just like you were before. There will be no trace, no mark, nothing."
>
> That, it seems, is her solution.
>
> She swathes me up in very tight, very uncomfortable bandages. Intricately she rolls them and ties them. She gives me to understand that this is usually an extra. She charges a great deal for this as a rule.
>
> "I do this better than anyone in the whole of Paris," she says. "Better than any doctor, better than any of those people who advertise, better than anyone in the whole of Paris."
>
> And I lie there in these damned bandages for a week. And there he lies, swathed up too, like a little mummy. And never crying.
>
> But now I like taking him in my arms and looking at him. A lovely forehead, incredibly white, the eyebrows drawn very faintly in gold dust. . . .
>
> Well, this was a funny time. (The big bowl of coffee in the morning with a pattern of red and blue flowers. I was always so thirsty.) But uneasy, uneasy. . . . Ought a baby to be as pretty as this, as pale as this, as silent as this? The other babies yell from morning to night. Uneasy. . . .
>
> When I complain about the bandages she says: "I promise you that when you take them off you'll be just as you were before." And it is true. When she takes them off there is not one line, not one wrinkle, not one crease.
>
> And five weeks afterwards there I am, with not one line, not one wrinkle, not one crease.

And there he is, lying with a ticket tied round his wrist because he died in hospital. And there I am looking down at him, without one line, without one wrinkle, without one crease. . . . (pp.51–2)

In this most moving of passages, the tragedy of the situation is brought out by the off-setting of the death of the baby with the nurse's concern for the vanity of her patient. Characteristically, the irony is implied, never directly stated. Even the mercenary streak which normally tempts the nurse to make a charge for this service is suppressed by her on this occasion. And yet, the very suggestion of beauty being conceived of as a commodity cheapens the whole notion of it. Certainly, this interest in the commercial potential of vanity is found wanting when it is set against the genuine beauty of a vulnerable baby, so delicately drawn by the narrator. But perhaps the most powerful narrative stroke connected with the idea of this contrast is the symbolic use to which she puts the visual image of the bandages. A comparison is drawn between the wrappings into which the nurse 'swathes' Sasha for reasons of restoring her physical attractiveness, and the swaddling clothes into which the newly-born infant is also 'swathed'. This construction permits the image of the 'mummy', which technically applies specifically to the baby, to apply both to the baby, because he resembles an Egyptian corpse, and to Sasha too, because she is the baby's mother. In a way, the image works in the manner of a transferred epithet, although the meaning is made more complex by the suggestion of death which it conveys. The pathos of the image as it applies to the baby is appreciated on the realisation that his untimely death will prevent him from reaching the age when he would be able to utter the word 'Mummy'. And this image is important too for adding to the powerful anticipation of his death which operates throughout the passage, and which is initiated implicitly through a symbolic suggestion as early as the nurse's first remarks: 'There will be no trace, no mark, nothing.' That the concept of 'nothing' covers the existence of the baby himself, is not appreciated by the nurse, and it is not immediately comprehended by the reader either. And yet the narrator, recounting in retrospect despite the use of the present tense, is aware of the ironic potential of the word. To the concept, she soon attaches a development which will become haunting through a triple repetition of it – 'not one line, not one wrinkle, not one crease.' These are the words which account for much of the distance and control of the writing.

The mummification of Sasha, which is depicted symbolically in the bandages applied to her after the birth of her baby, suggests that death touches her too. And in the visits which she makes through memory to scenes from the past, we are given an insight into some of the possible causes of her disillusionment with and withdrawal from involvement in human relationships. Undoubtedly, the unhappy experience of being abandoned by her husband, Enno, when at her most emotionally vulnerable – at the onset of her pregnancy – must have had a profound effect on her. In the evocation of the scene, however, the narrative lays no blame, leaving the reader to interpret the implications of the situation. But again, by the very reserve and control which is exercised in the rendering of what must have been a very painful experience, the effect of the suffering is actually augmented:

"You don't know how to make love," he said. That was about a month after we got to Paris. "You're too passive, you're lazy, you bore me. I've had enough of this. Goodbye."

He walked out and left me alone – that night and the next day, and the next night and the next day. With twenty francs on the table. And I'm sure now that I'm going to have a baby, though I haven't said a word about it.

I have to go out to get myself something to eat. The patron knows, the patronne knows, everybody knows. . . . Waking up at night, listening, waiting. . . .

The third day I make up my mind that he isn't coming back. A blue day. This is the first time that I look at the patronne instead of sliding past her with my eyes down. She inquires about Monsieur. Monsieur may be away for some time.

Blue sky over the streets, the houses, the bars, the cafés, the vegetable shops and the Faubourg Montmartre. . . .

I buy milk, a loaf of bread, four oranges, and go back to the hotel.

Squeezing the rind of an orange and smelling the oil. A lot of oil – they must be pretty fresh. . . . I think: "What's going to happen?" After all, I don't much care what happens. And just as I am thinking this Enno walks in with a bottle of wine under his arm.

"Hello," he says.

"I've got some money," he says. "My God, isn't it hot? Peel me an orange."

"I'm very thirsty," he says. "Peel me an orange."

Now is the time to say "Peel it yourself," now is the time to say "Go to hell," now is the time to say "I won't be treated like this." But much too strong – the room, the street, the thing in myself, oh, much too strong. . . . I peel the orange, put it on a plate and give it to him.

He says; "I've got some money."

He brings out a mille note, a second mille note. I don't ask where he has got them. Why ask? Money circulates; it circulates – and how! Why, you wouldn't believe it sometimes.

He pours me a glass of wine. "It's fresh. I've kept it away from the sun."

"But your hands are so cold," he says. "My girl. . . ."

He draws the curtains to keep the sun out.

When he kissed my eyelids to wake me it was dark. (pp.107–8)

Despite the economy of the text, and possibly even because of it, the nature of the relationship between Sasha and her husband is brought out most powerfully in this extract. The discourse presents the facts with no narrative indictment of the injustice of the situation. And yet the reader cannot fail to see the blatant inequality in the relationship, together with the oppressiveness of male domination and female dependence. Sasha's own narrative reticence on the subject of the emotional wound inflicted by Enno's rejection of her is characteristic of her. The pain, however, is evoked stylistically through the blandness of the text at this point, which manages to create the effect of shock. It is in her expression of the duration of his absence – the singulative listing of a series of units of time connected monotonously with the same conjunction 'and', rather than an iterative summary – that we feel the strength of her own overwhelming dumbfoundedness at what has befallen her. And shock, too, is evident in the incomplete grammatical syntax of the 'sentence' which expresses the financial straits in which he has left her. This utterance, lacking a main verb, creates the impression that it is a mere appendix. However, its appearance in the text as a separate unit bestows upon it the status of independence, and our attention is drawn to it thereby. In fact, it does have a great deal to contribute to the development of the idea of inequality in the marriage, for Sasha's plight highlights the root of oppressive patriarchal relationships in which the woman is also dependent upon the man for her material and physical well-being. The additional information about her pregnancy, which is attached to this statement by its commencement with the conjunction 'And', exacerbates her dilemma in the respect that even greater financial, as well as emotional, support is necessary at such a time.

Wisely, Sasha avoids dwelling too much on her depression, by occupying herself with the practical necessities of buying food. In this way, she is forced to leave her room, and so to confront others. Again, her emotions are implied stylistically rather than directly in the text. Now it is her embarrassment which is suggested, by the three-fold repetition of 'knows'. The ellipsis marks cut short the expression of this awkward feeling, and diegetic time is eclipsed until night-time when the use of the present participle in the description of her response on 'waking up' creates a sense of eternity about her desire to have Enno back.

It is not until the 'third day' that Sasha accepts the fact that her husband's return is unlikely. Still the expression of her emotion is relentlessly economical. The employment of an impersonal metaphor to convey her depression in the briefest of phrases is all that we are given: 'A blue day.' But a change in her attitude to other people is noted when she is now able to meet the patronne face to face, although she is still evasive in her explanation of her husband's whereabouts – 'Monsieur may be away for some time.' The formality of this assertion stems any further questions on the subject, and thus she avoids an involvement in a long explanation.

The concept of 'blue' which was used in the metaphor is now transferred by pathetic fallacy to her description of the scene which confronts her on her walk. Again, the description appears bland, consisting of a mere inventory of places, but the lack of any imaginative embellishment of this scene by the narrator who perceives it, is evidence of her mood. The basic list of her purchases too, develops the idea that she is, at the moment, incapable of transcending her depression. In her own words, rendered a little late, she doesn't 'much care what happens', and the power of the text rests on its ability to convey this feeling of indifference stylistically, as we have seen.

Enno's reappearance at the moment when she has accepted her lot is, of course, full of irony. The cornucopian symbol of the 'bottle of wine under his arm' makes for a direct contrast to the humble fare of milk, bread and oranges, to which Sasha was reduced in his absence. He has returned in the role of provider, and for this he expects domestic service and sexual favours, both of which he receives before the passage is ended. The arrogance of his opening words to his wife displays no sign of an apology or even any sense of an explanation. Instead, his declaration that he has 'money' with him, and his demand for a peeled orange, make it quite clear that he feels entitled to behave as he will. Sasha's initial response to this bullish attitude brings her close to rebellion, and for the first time in the passage we see her reserve and control falter. But the moment passes, and characteristically her sense of indignation remains unexpressed. Feeling the pressure of other needs weighing heavily upon her, she concedes. The discourse, however, reflects her emotional struggle through her actual silence. All the direct speech belongs to Enno. No verbal response is made to his statements, and this is most noticeable when he repeats his assertion that he has brought money with him. Sasha's taciturn compliance with his will suggests much about the oppression in the relationship. Even the reconciliation in bed, which is suggested by a textual ellipsis, is not what it seems. Immediately prior to this moment, Enno hands Sasha a glass of wine, symbolically thereby claiming his right as provider to have sexual intercourse with her. The physical union occurs in the darkness, Enno having shut out the light, and a darkness induced through sleep is Sasha's re- sponse to the act. Perhaps her withdrawal from the desire to formulate emotional relationships begins here, and the process of mummification is set in motion.

By contrast, Sasha's relationship with René, the gigolo, whom she meets some nineteen years after the event described in the passage above,[3] is based on a similar system of patronage, although this time it is she who has the money and he who relies upon her for it. This arrangement in itself provides Sasha with the independence which she had lacked in her earlier relationship with Enno. We notice the caution with which she plans out the logistics of the money required for the evening with René, and her care to take a little more than necessary should she need to exert that independence and pay for a taxi home:

> I have sixteen hundred francs left. Enough to pay for the dress I chose today, enough to pay my hotel bill and the journey back to London. How much over? Say four hundred francs. I take two

hundred and fifty. Two hundred francs for the meal, if there is a meal; fifty francs behind the mirror at the back of my handbag, for a taxi home in case we quarrel, in case he turns nasty. "Hey, taxi" – and you're out of everything. (p.128)

Needless to say, the impecunious gigolo is quick to accept Sasha's offer of dinner, his only worry being one of appearances, for the sake of which he asks her to give him the money before they enter the restaurant:

> I give him the two hundred francs and the corners of his mouth go down.
> "When you've settled up – dinner, drinks, taxis," I say, "there'll be about two francs left. I planned it out."
> "Oh, ce qu'elle est rosse, cette femme!" (p.130)

The importance of money to Sasha in the establishment of her independence is stressed by the amount of narrative time which is spent on the subject. As for René, he makes a career out of chasing rich women in order that they may provide for him. Having earlier mistaken Sasha's fur coat for the symbol of wealth, he allowed himself to become involved with her. Here, his exaggerated gesture of disappointment with the small amount of money she hands over to him, is taken by Sasha in good part. By now she is used to and even amused by his scheming. Her knowledge of her own limited resources allows her to enjoy this relationship in a way which would not be possible if it were to follow the pattern of oppressor/oppressed. By now, he too must realise that her means are small, and yet in spite of this he continues to want to develop their relationship, convinced that Sasha brings him 'luck'.[4] Clearly, his response rendered in the quotation above shows him playing the role of disappointed gigolo with some deliberate comic effect.

Gradually, in spite of herself, through becoming involved with René, Sasha's nineteen-year mummification begins to wear away. He has an effect on her which she finds difficult to define:

> I don't know what it is about this man that seems to me so natural, so gay – that makes me also feel natural and happy, just as if I were young – but really young. I've never been young. When I was young I was strained-up, anxious. I've never been really young. I've never played.

Certainly, we have witnessed the 'strained-up' anxiety of her younger day; the passage in which Enno temporarily rejected her demonstrated this aspect of her personality well. But her re-emergence into an affective life from the death which has suppressed her emotions for so long, is not achieved without pain and some more anxiety too. René, who wants to make love to her, cannot understand her excuse that she is afraid, and through his questioning he tries to make her look at herself, to examine her own fear, thereby to dispel it:

> "Afraid," he says, "afraid! But what are you afraid of? . . . You think I'll strangle you, or cut your throat for the sake of that beautiful ring of yours. Is that it?"
> "No, I'm sure you wouldn't kill me to get my ring."
> "Then perhaps you are afraid I'll kill you, not because I want money, but because I like to do bad things. But that's where you're so stupid. With you, I don't want to do bad things."
> "There's always the one that you don't want to do bad things with, isn't there?"
> "Yes, there's always the one," he says. "I want to lie close to you and feel your arms round me."
> – And tell me everything, everything. . . . He has said that bit before. (pp.143–4)

Sasha's feeling of discomfort is evident in the cynicism with which she responds to the deliberate extravagance of his utterances. Of course she is not afraid for her physical well-being, but she shies away from bringing the root of her anxiety out into the open. René's questioning, however, is relentless, and at last Sasha's defences are worn down by it:

> "Then what are you afraid of? Tell me. I'm interested. Of men, of love? . . . What, still? . . . Impossible."
> You are walking along a road peacefully. You trip. You fall into blackness. That's the past – or perhaps the future. And you know that there is no past, no future, there is only this blackness, changing faintly, slowly, but always the same.
> "You want to know what I'm afraid of? All right, I'll tell you. . . . I'm afraid of men – yes, I'm very much afraid of men. And I'm even more afraid of women. And I'm very much afraid of the whole bloody human race. . . . Afraid of them?" I say. "Of

course I'm afraid of them. Who wouldn't be afraid of a pack of damned hyenas?"

Thinking: "Oh, shut up. Stop it. What's the use?" But I can't stop. I go on raving.

"And when I say afraid – that's just a word I use. What I really mean is that I hate them. I hate their voices, I hate their eyes, I hate the way they laugh. . . . I hate the whole bloody business. It's cruel, it's idiotic, it's unspeakably horrible. I never had the guts to kill myself or I'd have got out of it long ago. So much the worse for me. Let's leave it at that."

. . . I know all about myself now, I know. You've told me so often. You haven't left me one rag of illusion to clothe myself in. But by God, I know what you are too, and I wouldn't change places. . . .

Everything spoiled, all spoiled. Well, don't cry about it. No, I won't cry about it. . . . But may you tear each other to bits, you damned hyenas, and the quicker the better. . . . Let it be destroyed. Let it happen. Let it end, this cold insanity. Let it happen.

Only five minutes ago I was in the Deux Magots, dressed in that damned cheap black dress of mine, giggling and talking about Antibes, and now I am lying in a misery of utter darkness. Quite alone. No voice, no touch, no hand. . . . How long must I lie here? For ever? No, only for a couple of hundred years this time, miss. . . . (pp.144–5)

In this critical scene, the painful process of awakening in Sasha is begun. The final straw for her is provided by René's disbelief that a woman of her age can possibly 'still' be afraid of love. In her private response to this she implicitly challenges the whole notion of age and experience, setting those temporarily conditioned ideas against a terrifying vision of timelessness. Her use of metaphorical language allows her to present abstract concepts in a way which is dramatically effective. Thus, the sudden facing up to this void at the centre of life is linked to the sensation of falling, on a previously tranquil walk, into a state of 'blackness'. On the level of the diegesis, this comparison refers to the feelings of happiness which René had stimulated in her becoming disrupted by the obligation to face those questions of central importance which she has so far managed to keep at the back of her mind. But a further implication may be appreciated in that the qualification of this 'blackness' as 'the past' suggests that the peaceful walk refers to her meanderings in Paris during which she has tried to recapture the past. In that respect, when the concept of time, which this 'blackness' is said to represent, becomes indistinguishable – 'the past – or perhaps the future' – then the vision which the metaphors imply becomes terrifying, in the sense that time as we know it is expunged.

Sasha chooses not to share this metaphysical anxiety with René, preferring, for his benefit, to translate it into the less difficult question of a fear of people. But her utterances take on a definite tone of rhetoric, suggesting an element of persuasiveness in her voice, which conceals as much as it conveys. A rhetorical question sets the tone of the first of her two speeches. In answer to it, she presents a climactic arrangement of elements which begins with an assertion of her fear of 'men'. This assertion is qualified in the second part of the declaration in which she embraces within the category a fear of 'women' too. In this way, the nature of her anxiety is shown to be more complex than the mere sexual fear which René may have taken her initial observation to have suggested. Carefully, Sasha works towards the climax of the series, which is now realised with a closing flourish – 'And I'm very much afraid of the whole bloody human race.' A momentary pause, indicated by the ellipsis marks, makes for dramatic effect before the speech continues with another rhetorical question. Now, the idea of her fear of the human race is developed with a most apposite image of 'a pack of damned hyenas', which perfectly crystalises the theme of the unsympathetic laughter of others.[5]

In the narrative arrangement of this final part of the first speech, Sasha's flow of rhetoric is underlined when, between the question 'Afraid of them?' and its answer, she places the directive 'I say'. This manoeuvre creates the impression that the narrator is making the most of her full flight of rhetoric, and is possibly even sending it up a little. There is a definite sense of ambivalence in her attitude to what she is saying and the way in which she is saying it. Clearly, the rhetoric is not empty. Throughout the novel she has made it plain that she feels uncomfortable in the presence of other people, especially strangers who, she feels, regard her with hostility. Nevertheless, some self-irony does seem to be present in the narrative at this point, and self-criticism is clearly seen in the term 'raving' through which she privately sums up her vocal performance. Even the appeal to her to 'shut up', which is made by the voice of reason, has no effect in stemming the flow of the oratory.

Instead, she launches into a new development with a second speech, in which she moves on from notions of fear to embrace those of hatred. Now, the use of rhetorical questions is dropped, and as a result, an intensity of tone is established which transcends any self-consciousness inherent in the handling of the style. Undoubtedly, the change of tack which allows her to express her emotion more genuinely, assists in achieving this depth of feeling.

On the conclusion of the direct speech, uttered aloud vaguely in the direction of the invisible René, Sasha continues by developing an internal dialogue, using the device of the split into two voices. At first, some ambiguity of reference is engendered when it is unclear to whom the use of the second person singular applies in these three concluding paragraphs. The context of the first paragraph, in which Sasha bemoans the fact that this person has destroyed the illusions about herself, seems to suggest that the narratee is René. Indeed, it is through him that she has been forced to examine herself. The final derogatory line seems to point towards the gigolo too, whom Sasha mentally insults by inferring that if she is disappointed in herself then he has even more reason to be disappointed in himself – 'But by God, I know what you are too, and I wouldn't change places. . . .'

In the second paragraph, Sasha stands back a little, for a moment only, to assess that everything has been 'spoiled'. Again, it seems likely that she refers to the loss of the harmonious atmosphere which had been built up between them. Now, the split in the voices emerges most clearly with a comment and a response, each element of which is entirely her own: 'Well, don't cry about it. No, I won't cry about it. . . .' This schism is, by now, quite familiar to us. Its presence here, however, does increase the ambiguity of the use of 'you' which normally becomes part of that process of division, being a term by which one half of the voice refers to the other. In this particular paragraph, however, following the elipsis marks there is a change in the level of consciousness when the 'you' which was previously applied to René now becomes directed to the human race. The identification mark is, of course, in the imagery: 'But may you tear each other to bits, you damned hyenas, and the quicker the better. . . .' Still within the same paragraph, a further alteration in the level of consciousness is indicated after the second set of ellipsis marks when there is a change to the imperative mood with a series of commands all of which begin with 'Let'. Thus, the paragraph which had begun on a note of dejection, ends with yet another rhetorical flourish, although this time the oratory remains internalised within the confines of Sasha's own mind.

In the final paragraph, again Sasha stands back for a moment to assess the decline in her mood over the last 'five minutes'. Her assertion that she is now 'quite alone' is, of course, not intended literally. Obviously, René is still with her in the room, but he is powerless to bring her out of her 'misery of utter darkness'. Indeed, all that she is left with is the company provided by that schism in her own voice, and even that dialogue, ironically, takes on a most formal tone with the use of 'miss' now replacing the more familiar 'you'. In its final comment, the second voice refers by implication to the earlier period of barrenness in Sasha's life, through the words 'this time': 'How long must I lie here? For ever? No, only for a couple of hundred years this time, miss. . . .' The flippancy of tone here highlights the meaninglessness of any human conception of time when seen against the background of that terrifying vision of 'blackness', as this is. And so in the ending we are brought back, through implication, to that sense of despair which overshadows and motivates the entire passage.

At the end of this extract, Sasha sums up the inconceivability of union between herself and René when she reduces him, through her use of terminology, to the status of a common prostitute: 'I heave myself out of the darkness, slowly, painfully. And there I am, and there he is, the poor gigolo.' Clearly, she feels that he is unable to assist her in coming to terms with her own sense of despair, and in his subsequent behaviour he displays a total lack of comprehension of her dilemma by attempting to elicit her pity for his own physical 'wounds' in an effort to seduce her. And yet, between this point in the diegesis and the end of the novel, there is a change of attitude on Sasha's part, which comes about through an enlightening dramatic incident, and results in her willingness to reciprocate his sexual passion.

In the closing pages of the novel, both Sasha's attitude to René – her reduction of his status to that of a prostitute – and the split in her voice, play an important part in building up the *progression d'effet* towards the final ironic outcome of the work. Firstly, having already refused his overture of sexual affection – 'rien à faire' (p.147) – she subsequently changes her mind after he has taken her back to the hotel. It is at this point, however, when they begin to 'kiss each other fervently' (p.148), that the schism which has so far restricted itself to the domain of her mental voice, and of which she has not seemed to be self-conscious, asserts itself with more authority to cause her anxiety: 'I am uneasy, half of myself somewhere else.' This awareness, together with an argumentative temper stimulated by the effect of too much alcohol, serves to alter her mood into one of mistrust: 'He looks méchant, he could be méchant, this man.' (p.152). However, it is not until she is in close physical contact with René that she feels at her most vulnerable:

> I feel his hard knee between my knees. My mouth hurts, my breasts hurt, because it hurts, when you have been dead, to come alive. . . . (p.153)

Clearly, the mummification process has been put into reverse, and, as I suggested earlier, the re-awakening of desire in Sasha is not effected without some considerable pain. It is at this point that the second voice comes into play in an effort to protect her from emotional involvement, and in this function it creates much dramatic tension when a conflict arises between it and Sasha's newly-revived desire to succumb to the feelings which are welling up inside her:

> "Now everything's going to be all right," he says.
> "T'as compris?" he says.
> Of course, the ritual answer is "Si, j'ai compris. . . ."
> I lie there, thinking "Yes I understand." Thinking "For the last time." Thinking nothing. Listening to a high, clear, cold voice. My voice.
> "Of course I understand. Naturally I understand. I should be an awful fool if I didn't. If you look in the right-hand pocket of the dressing-case over on that table you'll find the money you want."
> He lets go of my wrists. I feel him go very still.
> "It isn't locked. Take the thousand-franc note. But for God's sake leave me the others, or I'll be in an awful jam."
> But how heavy he is, how much heavier than one would have thought. . . .
> "You mustn't think," I say, "that I'm vexed about anything, because I'm not. Everybody's got their living to earn, haven't they? I'm just trying to save you a lot of trouble."

Don't listen, that's not me speaking. Don't listen. Nothing to do with me – I swear it. . . .

"And I thought you were awfully sweet to me," I say. "I loved all the various stories you told me about yourself. Especially that one about your wounds and your scars – that amused me very much."

I put my arm up over my face, because I have a feeling that he is going to hit me.

"I'm just trying to save you a whole lot of trouble," I say, "a whole lot of waste of time. You can have the money right away, so it would be a waste of time, wouldn't it?"

His weight is not on me any longer. He is standing up. He has moved so quickly that I haven't had time to put my arms around him, or to say "Stay", to say "Don't do this, don't leave me like this, don't."

"Yes, you're right," he says. "It would be a waste of time."

"You and your wounds – don't you see how funny you are? You did make me laugh. Other people's wounds – how funny they are! I shall laugh every time I think about you. . . ." (pp.153–4)

Sasha's lack of response to René's optimistic comment, which prompts the question 'T'as compris?', is ominous. Already there is conflict in her mind, and this is shown in the irony within her mental recognition that there is a 'ritual' answer. Gradually, the hint of cynicism which is apparent in this observation will become stronger as the second voice is given a free rein and allowed to emerge through actual utterances. From the beginning, however, Sasha implicitly dissociates herself from this cynicism. Her attitude is shown in the detachment which is evident in the line – 'Listening to a high, clear, cold voice. My voice.' It is at this point that the second voice takes over, and, for the first time in the novel, it is allowed to find breath. Through this important development, the dramatic tension of the scene is augmented. Now, instead of suffering all the pain herself, it is Sasha who, through the device of the second voice, finds the power to inflict pain on somebody else. René's responses are most powerfully conveyed. The focal point does not fall on him directly, but his reactions are suggested by the way in which Sasha registers her own awareness of him. Thus, in the most economical manner, a detailed picture of the shock of suffering personal rejection is drawn:

> He lets go of my wrists. I feel him go very still. . . .
>
> But how heavy he is, how much heavier than one would have thought. . . .
>
> I put my arm up over my face, because I have a feeling that he is going to hit me. . . .
>
> His weight is not on me any longer. He is standing up. He has moved so quickly. . . . (p.153)

Clearly, the second voice has hit home, and the laconicism with which he expresses his feelings of dejection leaves the reader with a most acute image of the pain of being utterly crushed: '"Yes, you're right," he says. "It would be a waste of time."' Set against this economy is the relentlessness of the utterances which pour forth from Sasha, and over which she seems to have no control. Her own experience of pain is suggested by the internal riot in operation within her mind – her powerlessness to overcome the increasing cynicism of those utterances which are in direct conflict with her desire for love: 'Don't listen, that's not me speaking. Don't listen. Nothing to do with me – I swear it. . . .' The irony of the technique employed in this passage is seen in the evident reversal which has taken place. In this way, the cynicism which, until now, has been suppressed by Sasha, is given voice, while her natural timidity is the element which is now suppressed.

Developing from the sense of detachment which was evident in Sasha's attitude to the second voice, there now comes an even more definite sense of alienation from it, which is suggested technically in the allocation to it of the third-person pronouns – 'her' and 'she'. In the preamble to the emergence of this completely separate entity, Sasha focuses on her crisis of personal identity:

> When he has gone I turn over on my side and huddle up, my knees almost touching my chin. I cry in the way that hurts right down, that hurts your heart and your stomach. Who is this crying? The same one who laughed on the landing, kissed him and was happy. This is me, this is myself, who is crying. The other – how do I know who the other is? She isn't me. (p.154)

When 'the other' does emerge, the limits of her utterances are demarcated by quotation marks. Thus, she is even further separated from the self with whom Sasha instinctively identifies:

Her voice in my head: "Well, well, well, just think of that now. What an amusing ten days! Positively packed with thrills. The last performance of What's-her-name And Her Boys or It Was All Due To An Old Fur Coat. Positively the last performance. . . . Go on, cry, allez-y. Encore. Tirez, as they say here. . . . Now calm, calm, say it all out calmly. You've had dinner with a beautiful young man and he kissed you and you've paid a thousand francs for it. Dirt cheap at the price, especially with the exchange the way it is. Don't forget the exchange, dearie – but of course you wouldn't would you? And you've picked up one or two people in the street and you've bought a picture. Don't forget the picture, to remind you of – what was it to remind you of? Oh, I know – of human misery. . . ." (pp.154–5)

The mocking irony of the voice serves as a cynical commentary on the events of the diegesis. No doubt the metaphor of the play arises from Sasha's subliminal memory of René's accusation that she loves 'playing a comedy' (p.150). But his accusation in itself does seem to point to a tendency in Sasha towards self-dramatisation. We have already appreciated the conscious use of rhetoric in some of her utterances; now, using the device of the second voice, she appears to be exposing, by parodying, her own awareness of that theatricality. And yet, the significance of both the very real dilemma which is expressed in the paragraph immediately preceding this one, and the undoubted suffering which she has endured at certain times in her life and is enduring now, is not diminished thereby. Indeed, if anything, the complexity of the dilemma is augmented by its juxtaposition to this element of cynicism.

The second voice also has an important part to play in the development of the diegesis. Firstly, it is responsible for drawing attention to 'the man next door', in preparation for the final débâcle of the text:

She says: "I hate to stop you crying. I know it's your favourite pastime, but I must remind you that the man next door has probably heard every damned thing that's happened and is now listening-in to the sequel. Not exactly what one would have expected, perhaps. But still – quite amusing." (p.155)

This is the eighth brief reference to 'the commis', whose significance in the novel will become all too apparent in the closing

lines. Following this reference to him, and joined to that utterance
by a conjunction, comes a suggestion that René may have taken all
of Sasha's remaining money: '"And another thing," she says. "If
he's taken all the money – which he almost certainly has – that'll be
a lovely business, won't it?"' This thought encourages Sasha to
check, and when she does so she discovers that she has, indeed,
misjudged the 'chic gigolo' (p.156) on this point. Her recognition of
what she takes to be his ultimate sincerity delights her, and, in
celebration of it, she toasts him with whisky. The liberating effect
of the alcohol has an important part to play in the climax of the
novel. Through it, she manages to free herself from the second
voice:

> I have another drink. Damned voice in my head, I'll stop you
> talking. . . .
>
> I am walking up and down the room. She has gone. I am
> alone. (p.157)

With the cynicism of that voice removed, the check on Sasha's
dreams and motivations vanishes:

> I think: "How awful I must look! I must put the light out."
> But it doesn't matter. Now I am simple and not afraid; now I
> am myself. He can look at me if he wants to. I'll only say: "You
> see, I cried like that because you went away." (p.158)

The recovery of her 'simple' perception, her unified vision rather
than the divided outlook which had plagued her earlier, does not,
however, succeed in diminishing all her ambivalent feelings. This
is made clear in a subsequent utterance which qualifies the above
assertion: '(Or did I cry like that because I'll never sing again,
because the light in my sale cerveau has gone out?)'. A hint of
regret may be detected in this alternative reason for her tears, but
the use of the brackets signifies that the thought remains subordinated to the main flow of the text. Now, as though to keep that fear
at bay, Sasha bends all of her imaginative powers towards evoking
in her mind the scene of René's return. This is what she wants
above everything else, for now she will be able to give herself to
him:

Now he has come up to the hotel.

He presses the button and the door opens.

He is coming up the stairs.

Now the door is moving, the door is opening wide. I put my arms over my eyes.

He comes in. He shuts the door after him.

I lie very still, with my arm over my eyes. As still as if I were dead. . . . (pp.158–9)

A similarity between the position adopted here – 'my arm over my eyes' – and that adopted by her in the preceding scene with René, when she was afraid that he might hit her, has disturbing implications. Firstly, it reminds us of the pain and humiliation which she had inflicted on him, an experience not likely to lead to his return, and secondly, it is a sign of withdrawal from a full engagement in what may follow. And yet, as the final lines make clear, Sasha does not withdraw from the outcome of the scene. After an ellipsis of an indefinite amount of diegetic time, she demonstrates her intuitive knowledge that it is not René who has come into the room, but the hateful 'commis' whom she has despised throughout her time in Paris:

I don't need to look, I know.

I think: "Is it the blue dressing-gown, or the white one? That's very important. I must find that out – it's very important."

I take my arm away from my eyes. It is the white dressing-gown.

He stands there, looking down at me. Not sure of himself, his mean eyes flickering.

He doesn't say anything. Thank God, he doesn't say anything. I look straight into his eyes and despise another poor devil of a human being for the last time. For the last time. . . .

Then I put my arms round him and pull him down on to the bed, saying: "Yes – yes – yes. . . ." (p.159)

The removal of her arm from her eyes signifies her full acknowledgement of the reality of the situation, and her ultimate gesture of pulling him towards her initiates the act. Thus, Sasha is not forced into anything; she meets this man in a sexual embrace of her own free will. But there is something deeply disturbing in the portrait of this man, who is drawn negatively throughout the novel, and here too, with his 'mean eyes'. It is difficult to accept Sasha's belief that she despises 'another poor devil of a human being for the last time.' No doubt, René's unexpected gesture, which so surprised her, has inspired in her the illusion that a positive, mutual relationship between a man and a woman is conceivable after all. But the narrative itself points out her own awareness of the fragility of this dream by focusing on the relief that she feels when the commis 'doesn't say anything'. The reader is left to contemplate what might have happened had he spoken. Would his words have brought her back to the reality of the situation – that a sexual involvement with a man who cannot see beyond the physical epitomises everything that frightens her most about the organisation of 'the whole bloody human race' (p.144). The grim irony of Sasha's Joycean affirmation, with which the novel ends, leaves us in no doubt at all about 'the misery of utter darkness' (p.145) which will follow this final desperate plea for emotional fulfilment.

In this novel, Jean Rhys gives an acute new angle to the oppressive nature of the patriarchal system in which a woman is financially dependent upon a man. Sasha's economic independence in her relationship with René, the gigolo, inverts the usual gender order. Logically, his position should recall her own former dependence upon her husband, Enno. It doesn't, of course. Rhys's suggestion of the inequality in that relationship is so acute that, by comparison to it, René's 'dependence' upon Sasha must be viewed as a mere travesty. By the same token, Edward's financial dependence upon Antoinette in *Wide Sargasso Sea* does not bring about any gender reversal in the roles of oppressor/oppressed. In my examination of this final novel, I should now like to show how Rhys demonstrates the tragedy of a system in which Antoinette's sense of oppression can find relief only through her escape into madness.

6

Antoinette and Edward: Locating the Tragic Figure

In *Wide Sargasso Sea*, a tragic intensity which is unique in the canon of Jean Rhys's writing, is evoked through the alternation of two distinct voices in the text. Antoinette Cosway, the last 'Rhys woman', shares the narrative discourse with her husband, Edward Rochester, whose picture of himself as a tragic hero can be shown to have been carefully striven for. In this final chapter, by focusing on these two contrasting self-portraits, I will demonstrate that whereas Edward's rendering of himself eventually defeats its object through its very intention, Antoinette does emerge as a genuine tragic figure.

Underlying the tragedy of Antoinette's situation is her powerlessness as an individual in the patriarchal environment in which she lives. As we have already seen, the part which money plays in the establishment of this sort of oppressive system is important, and I should like to give my exploration of Antoinette and Edward's potential for tragic stature a thematic focus by analysing the power of money to motivate and control these people's lives. The issue is a complex one, and in Rhys's handling of it she works through ambiguity to open up the question so that any distinction between the roles of oppressor and oppressed gradually becomes blurred.

There is a strong suggestion throughout the text that the moral decline of a 'gentle, generous' and 'brave'[1] soul such as Edward Rochester, may be traced to his materialism. This is shown to be a cultural value, and it is instilled into him at a very early age. Being the younger son of a wealthy father who, by leaving all his money to the elder, wishes to avoid weakening the family status, Edward is expected to contribute further to that status by taking part in an arranged marriage with a wealthy heiress. The pressure from his family is brought out constantly, in the form of letters which the unwilling Edward writes to his father. This, coupled with his own attitude of reluctance and bitterness, makes Edward into more of a victim of his own background than was suggested by the Bronte text. Certainly, Bronte's portrait of Edward Rochester in *Jane Eyre* lacks substance. In Rhys's text his character is considerably fleshed out so that his cruelty becomes understandable while, at the same time, just as unacceptable. Because Rhys allows the reader an insight into Edward's make-up and motivation, his behaviour is, to a certain extent, explained. Its cruelty is not ameliorated thereby, but it is, at least, observed to be a constituent element of his own human frailty – a fatal flaw in his personality.

But the social significance of money, its power to motivate and control people's lives, is shown to affect every character in the novel, regardless of status or colour. Christophine's position of independence is a challenge to culturally inherited values. Set against Antoinette's dependence upon her husband, the black woman's attitude to her own money presents a twentieth century image of financial liberation from male domination. This emerges clearly after her advice to Antoinette to leave Edward. The younger woman's reluctance to do so – 'He is my husband after all' – stimulates the following tirade against the failure of women to alter the social system:

> She spat over her shoulder. "All women, all colours, nothing but fools. Three children I have. One living in this world, each one a different father, but no husband, I thank my God. I keep my money. I don't give it to no worthless man." (p.91)

A tone of indignation and disgust is evoked dramatically by her gesture of spitting. For Christophine, the issues are human rather than racial, hence her criticism of women of 'all colours'. The repetition of the word 'all' brings out the universality of the matter. Her description of her own private life, insofar as it relates to her sexual relations with different men, places her very much ahead of her time. Her cynicism too, her dismissal of men as 'worthless', goes against the paternalistic myth current in those days, that the man, the head of the house, is the 'important person'.[2] It is likely that Christophine's cultural background, her first-hand experience of slavery, accounts for her sensitivity to other forms of oppression too.

The lack of any 'married woman's property Act'[3] ensures that Antoinette's money, on her marriage to Edward, becomes absorbed into his own estate. The injustice of this arrangement is demonstrated by Christophine's response when she learns that such a state of affairs prevails:

"But look me trouble, a rich white girl like you and more foolish than the rest. A man don't treat you good, pick up your skirt and walk out. Do it and he come after you."

"He will not come after me. And you must understand that I am not rich now, I have no money of my own at all, everything I had belongs to him."

"What you tell me there?" she said sharply.

"That is English law."

"Law! The Mason boy fix it, that boy worse than Satan and he burn in Hell one of these fine nights. . . ." (p.91)

Ignorant of English law she may be, but Christophine is no fool. She knows that some legal provision should have been drawn up in Antoinette's favour, and she is right to blame Richard Mason for this neglect of his step-sister's affairs. Her instinctive knowledge that Edward, himself, is not 'bad-hearted' is also correct. Early in his narrative it is made clear that he intends to rectify this situation, thus ensuring that Antoinette will be provided for. The passage in which he determines to do this, however, is also interesting for the insight it gives into Edward's own awareness of the oppressive forces which control his life. His reflections cast doubt on the idea of Antoinette as victim, and throw open the whole issue of buying and selling with regard to his own position in the arranged marriage:

Everything is too much, I felt as I rode wearily after her. Too much blue, too much purple, too much green. The flowers too red, the mountains too high, the hills too near. And the woman is a stranger. Her pleading expression annoys me. I have not bought her, she has bought me, or so she thinks. I looked down at the coarse mane of the horse ... Dear Father. The thirty thousand pounds have been paid to me without question or condition. No provision made for her (that must be seen to). I have a modest competence now. I will never be a disgrace to you or to my dear brother the son you love. No begging letters, no mean requests. None of the furtive shabby manoeuvres of a younger son. I have sold my soul or you have sold it, and after all

is it such a bad bargain? The girl is thought to be beautiful, she is
beautiful. And yet . . . (p.59)

The opening sentence shows Edward having adopted a subordinate position to Antoinette; it is he who follows her. His weariness
is reflected in his statement that 'Everything is too much'. This
expression usually has emotional connotations, and is often
uttered at a point of despair. But, through pathetic fallacy, the
development introduces a symbolic substitute for the causes of
Edward's fatigue. Thus, the oppressive effect of the natural landscape is made to stand in for the genuine cause of his distress. The
narrative arrangement of the substitution serves to slow up the
pace of the text as Edward focuses his thoughts on each colour in
turn, repeating the phrase 'too much' in a singulative pattern. At
first, the colours are abstracted from their context, but as the train
of thought develops, details of natural landscape are introduced to
create a setting for them. This sharpening of focus brings the real
reason for his feelings of disorientation into the picture. The
necessary connection between 'the woman' and the oppressive
force of nature is implied by the conjunction 'And'. The imperso-
nality of the expression, Edward's avoidance of Antoinette's name,
demonstrates his emotional distance from her, and this idea is
reinforced by the concept of 'a stranger' which he introduces to
describe her. But the distance is not sufficiently great to allow for
complete indifference on Edward's part. His assertion that her
expression 'annoys' him is evidence of that emotional engagement
which had been belied by the objectivity of the preceding sentence.
Thus, Edward's attitude of coolness towards her falters, and now
we approach the source of his misgivings.

When used to describe people, the metaphor of buying and
selling has inescapable historical significance. By being applied to
two Caucasians, as it is in this passage, the concept of slavery
which it implies is freed from its racial connections. In this way,
Jean Rhys opens up the whole issue, demonstrating that whereas
one form of oppression has come to an end, another, more sinister
form, is very much alive. The complexity of this current form of
slavery is suggested by the ambivalence which is apparent in the
following sentence: 'I have not bought her, she has bought me, or
so she thinks.' Again, it is the narrative presentation of the
utterance which is of key significance. The premise 'I have not
bought her', is developed by the assertion that 'she has bought

me'. This suggests that, to Edward, the issue is quite simple. However, with the unexpected addition of the ambiguous clause 'or so she thinks', the simplicity of the former two statements is suddenly cast into doubt. The roles of purchaser and purchased, or master and slave, are not clear-cut at all, and this uncertainty will be shown to characterise Edward's conception of his relationship with Antoinette throughout the novel.

A change in the level of the narrative is introduced by Edward's momentary alteration of focus, from these abstract matters to 'the coarse mane of the horse ...'. The ellipsis marks indicate the sudden transition, and with the words 'Dear Father', we are plunged into Edward's imagination as he composes a letter. The diegetic detail about the horse is important, for it economically keeps us in touch on the level of the story, and we are thus able to view Edward's misgivings in the context of this journey to the honeymoon house. This makes the content of his thoughts all the more foreboding, and our view of the incipient relationship between the young couple is affected. Clearly, at a time when he should be experiencing hope and the anticipation of a happy future, Edward's dissatisfaction and the feeling of bitterness which is about to emerge, are ill omens.

The device of the imagined letter to his father allows the full facts of the marriage settlement to emerge in the text. It also provides a medium by which Edward can express his bitterness about his family's expectations of him, and this is important for the extra dimension which it brings to his characterisation. As Christophine points out, he is 'not bad-hearted', and it is here that he makes clear his good intentions towards Antoinette. Again, however, the technical presentation is significant, for the use of brackets suggests that the assertion enclosed therein is subordinate to the main statement in the rest of the sentence. This modifies our perception of his words. Clearly, the narrative status of the bracketed intention implies that it is of less importance to him than the declaration of his own benefit from Antoinette's money. We are not surprised, therefore, that in the course of the novel he makes no further mention of this matter; presumably, he forgets, or neglects, to do anything about it.

The pressure exerted on Edward by his family is allowed to emerge in the ironic tone which he adopts when he speaks of them. No doubt, much jealousy of his brother taints that kindred relationship and makes the elder son less 'dear' to the younger than the latter's words declare. Antoinette's money has not only provided Edward with 'a modest competence' but, more importantly, it has given him what she has lost – complete financial independence. His freedom from the necessity of asking for money should also give him a self-respect which, no doubt, he had previously lacked. Such a lack is implied in the epithets 'begging' and 'mean'. His family too will have benefited from this new-found independence, for, with it, the threat of 'the furtive shabby manoeuvres of a younger son' is also removed. The form of a generalisation which this clause adopts demonstrates the cultural dimension underlying the practice of favouring the elder son. The implication is that the practice invariably encouraged the younger son to engage in underhand scheming. But the sense of self-respect which this freedom seems to imply disappears in the knowledge of what his action has cost him. In exchange for Antoinette's money, like Faustus, he has had to forfeit his 'soul'. Thus, the metaphor of buying and selling, a figure which springs from the commercial materialism of this world, is developed by being linked with a metaphysical concept, and the combination of these heterogeneous ideas serves both to clarify and to obscure the whole notion of advantage in the transaction. The beneficiary now appears to be Edward's father. This is suggested by the following clarification: '. . . or you have sold it.' And the terms of the contract have shifted too. The money has drifted out of focus, and the payment received for Edward's soul appears, now, to be Antoinette herself: '. . . and after all is it such a bad bargain? The girl is thought to be beautiful, she is beautiful.' The positive nature of the assertion is undermined by Edward's continued reluctance to use Antoinette's name, although a softening of attitude may be sensed in his alteration of reference from 'the woman' to 'the girl'. Nevertheless, the final words in the passage, interrupted by ellipsis marks – 'And yet . . .' – cloud any promise of a new awareness with suspicion. Clearly, Edward's misgivings have been transferred to doubts about Antoinette herself.

Connected to this particular financial transaction, a crowing cock becomes a recurring motif in the novel. Edward, himself, does not see the significance of it, but is sufficiently aware of it to report its presence in his narrative, and to recall that a similar sound had punctuated the silence of the previous night:

We mounted, turned a corner and the village was out of sight. A cock crowed loudly and I remembered the night before which we had spent in the town. Antoinette had a room to herself, she was exhausted. I lay awake listening to cocks crowing all night . . . (p.58)

Taking into consideration his subsequent conclusion that he has sold his soul, it would seem to be appropriate to regard the biblical significance of the crowing cock as intended here by the author. Certainly, that link is brought out later by Antoinette when, following her persuasion of Christophine to concoct a love-potion, she too, hears the crowing of a cock. Although, biblically, the cock is linked with Peter's denial of Christ, it is Judas's betrayal of him which immediately springs into Antoinette's mind:

Nearby a cock crowed and I thought, "That is for betrayal, but who is the traitor?" She did not want to do this. I forced her with my ugly money. And what does anyone know about traitors, or why Judas did what he did? (p.97)

The fact that the sound now impinges on Antoinette's conscious-ness where before it had been Edward's, suggests that it becomes a floating sign, not connected to one particular person in the novel. This factor adds to the ambiguity with which the question of guilt and betrayal is treated in the work. Antoinette's own ambivalence on the point is itself a sign of that uncertainty with which Jean Rhys achieves an open-ended structure rather than the closure of meaning associated with the classic realist text.

Antoinette's sensitivity to the significance of the crowing cock contrasts with Edward's own lack of insight. Towards the end of his narrative, as he prepares to leave the island prior to his ultimate denial of her – her incarceration in Thornfield Hall – he demon-strates this shortcoming in his own perceptiveness. In order to allow him social freedom when he arrives in England, it is important that he suppresses the fact of his marriage. To this end, he writes to his father, suggesting that 'the less you talk about my affairs, especially my marriage, the better.' (p.133). The crowing of the cock reinforces the suggestion of his link with Peter, for it occurs as he writes a second letter, to lawyers, in which he advises them to arrange accommodation for his arrival in Jamaica. He requires 'a furnished house, not too near the town, commodious enough to allow for two separate suites of rooms' and a staff of

servants prepared to be 'discreet' (p.134). The detail of the 'separate' rooms, which signifies the end of his sexual relationship with
Antoinette, recalls the ominous sleeping arrangements of the
wedding night.[4] Throughout the novel, the suggestion of inevitability about the failure of the marraige has contributed to the
tragic intensity of the tale. Now, as Edward's narrative draws to a
close, the tension increases with the relentlessness of the cock's
crowing. We recall that at this time, Antoinette, filled with despair,
lies in a drunken stupor in the bedroom:

> All the time I was writing this letter a cock crowed persistently
> outside. I took the first book I could lay my hands on and threw
> it at him, but he stalked a few yards away and started again.
> Baptiste appeared, looking towards Antoinette's silent room.
> "Have you got much more of this famous rum?"
> "Plenty rum," he said.
> "Is it really a hundred years old?"
> He nodded indifferently. A hundred years, a thousand all the
> same to *le bon Dieu* and Baptiste too.
> "What's that damn cock crowing about?"
> "Crowing for a change of weather."
> Because his eyes were fixed on the bedroom I shouted at him,
> "Asleep, dormi, dormi."
> He shook his head and went away. (p.134)

There is an interesting narrative anachrony which makes for a
particular discordance between the temporal orders of story and
narrative in Edward's version of the above events. I do not mean to
emphasise that usual type of discordance which is involved in any
retrospective mode of the telling and which is in operation here
too. Rather, I would like to focus on Edward's attention to order,
which actually manages to highlight the drama of the crowing cock
in spite of his lack of perception regarding its significance. The
phrase 'All the time" identifies the iterative mode of his comment
about the crowing cock. This sets up an immediate technical
contrast to the singulative mode which had been used in his
narrative rendering of the letter. Edward's assertion that these two
events – the writing of the letter and the crowing of the cock
– occupied the same diegetic time, and, indeed, occurred simultaneously, creates a tension between the two modes. The discordance results not only from the obvious opposition between

singulative and iterative styles of rendering, but also from the fact that the information about the cock is suspended in the narrative; it occupies a position later in the narrative order than its position within the order of the diegesis. This technical disruption, together with Edward's violent response in the diegesis, does result in more attention being drawn to the crowing than it would deserve were it not of some symbolic importance. We recall Antoinette's recognition of its significance, and as if to reinforce our response, Baptiste's behaviour acts as an indicator of the importance of remembering his absent mistress. Thanks to Baptiste, Antoinette's absence from this part of the text is physical only. As his gesture of 'looking towards Antoinette's silent room' makes clear, she is there in his mind as well as in the reader's. The transferred epithet used by Edward in this description gives a fascinating insight into his reluctance to face the truth. It is Antoinette who is 'silent' rather than the room, and she has become so because she has given herself up to the despair engendered by her realisation that she will never win Edward's love. In effect, it is he who has commanded this silence, and his intention to incarcerate her, to keep her existence a secret, demonstrates a desire to keep her silent forever. Our knowledge of the content of his letter makes this silence full of ominous significance. Baptiste's indifference to his master's conversation, and his relentless gazing towards Antoinette's room – 'his eyes were fixed on the bedroom' – serve to increase the portentousness of the entire scene. This passage is rich in suggestiveness. Every gesture, every word, conveys meaning above and beyond that of its surface significance. Thus, even Baptiste's words '"Crowing for a change of weather"', have an irony of which he, himself, cannot be fully aware.

Jean Rhys takes care to ensure that her use of biblical significance, seen above in the symbolic potential of the cock, is literary rather than religious. For a start, it is 'betrayal' rather than the biblically authentic 'denial' which is a particular focus in the text, and besides, Antoinette's questioning of the motives of Judas has already dispelled any suggestion that the Christian issues are clear-cut. Furthermore, the order of her words demonstrates that it is possible to recognise the sign as a symbol of betrayal, abstracted from any conscious Christian context. This is shown by her immediate response to the sound: 'That is for betrayal . . .'. The reference to Judas occurs almost as an afterthought. Likewise, the writer's focus upon the religious influence on Daniel Cosway, the most odious character in the novel, demonstrates that his response to biblical teachings is a response to their literary effect. Clearly, Daniel's life does not follow a Christian pattern. The principles of forgiveness and love are shown to be completely foreign to him, and yet we know that he reads the Bible 'every day' (p.81), and that he has even had the experience of being a 'preacher'.[5] Amélie hits the nail on the head when she states that 'he talk like a preacher' (p.100). Daniel's love of the Bible is defined by his love of rhetoric. His utterances are shot through with quotations from biblical texts, as, for example, this one which he directs to Edward:

> "When I hear you coming I take a good shot of rum, and then I take a glass of water to cool me down, but it don't cool me down, it run out of my eyes in tears and lamentations. . . ." (p.100)

The effect of the speech pattern in which Renaissance elegance combines with pidgin English is ironic, and the narrative portrait of Daniel as a whole is hostile. There are two reasons for this. Firstly, as we will see in a moment, his is a loathsome personality, and secondly, he has already engendered the hatred of Edward, in whose narrative he is portrayed.

Edward's animosity towards this man reveals itself on a subconscious level as well as a conscious one. Again, his text is rich in lateral meaning. Through the implications of familiar symbolic associations, he sets Daniel in a context which is suggestive of a medieval concept of hell:

> A large table covered with a red fringed cloth made the small room seem hotter; the only window was shut.
> "I put your chair near the door," Daniel said, "a breeze come in from underneath." But there was no breeze, not a breath of air, this place was lower down the mountain almost at sea-level.

The colour 'red', the heat, the lack of air, and the lower position of the house all hint at diabolic associations. But the portrait does not rely for its effect on suggestiveness only. Daniel's loathsomeness emerges for itself in his behaviour. His concept of God is of an Old Testament deity, a God full of vengeance and hostility:

> He went on talking, his eyes fixed on a framed text hanging on the dirty white wall, "Vengeance is Mine".

"You take too long, Lord," he told it. "I hurry you up a bit."
Then he wiped his thin yellow face and blew his nose on the
corner of the tablecloth. (pp.100–1)

Here, the detail of the 'dirty' state of the wall, and the unwhole-
some manner in which he abuses the tablecloth, speak for themselves; no narrative bias is needed to colour our response to this
disgusting man. His attitude to money too, establishes the corrupt-
ness of his nature, and in this respect he is placed in a class of his
own. We have already analysed Christophine's attitude to money,
and shown that even she is not unaffected by a certain materialism.
However, Christophine's value of money is put into a clearer
perspective when a distinct parallel is drawn between herself and
Daniel, and his attitude is found wanting by the implied comparison to hers. The parallel is suggested technically by a similar use of
phrasing to explain his choice of an independent life-style. These
words also echo those of Christophine so closely in content that we
cannot fail to make the link:

> The black and gilt clock on a shelf struck four.
> I must go. I must get away from his yellow sweating face and
> his hateful little room. I sat still, numb, staring at him.
> "You like my clock?" said Daniel. "I work hard to buy it. But
> it's to please myself. I don't have to please no woman. Buy me
> this and buy me that – demons incarnate in my opinion. . . ."
> (p.103)

It is the sentence 'I don't have to please no woman' which
technically recalls Christophine's assertion 'I don't give it to no
worthless man'. The double negative in each case is the mark of
identification. This grammatical irregularity anyway serves to
highlight each remark. But whereas we feel that Christophine's
view is born of the wisdom of experience – she has had three
children to support as well as herself – Daniel's motives for his
single life appear to spring from a selfish acquisitiveness which
precludes any desire to share. His wholly mercenary attitude is
brought out by his request for £500, in return for which he will
keep secret the facts of Antoinette's personal and family history. In
this respect, he is shown to differ most radically from Christophine
who refuses and is offended by Antoinette's offer of money in
exchange for the love-potion.[6] These two scenes are carefully

juxtaposed in order to bring out the contrasts between Christophine and Daniel. Christophine, loyal servant to Antoinette, and fond of her too, on a personal level, is disturbed by the young woman's distress. She wishes to help her because of her love for her – 'I do this foolishness because you beg me – not for money.' Daniel, on the other hand, sees himself in the role of malcontent. Carefully, he attempts to portray himself to Edward as the harshly treated illegitimate son of Antoinette's own father. In fact, his rendering is self-defeating, for it reveals, rather, how he himself is given to scheming and is bent on grasping as much money as he can from those whose personal circumstances make them vulnerable to blackmail. 'Old Cosway', as he calls Antoinette's father, was notorious for his extra-marital affairs and siring of mulattoes, and was therefore a perfect victim for Daniel to prey upon. Characteristically, Rhys allows the question of Daniel's true parentage to remain ambiguous. His own claim to be Cosway's son is disputed by the old man himself, who also casts doubt upon the integrity of Daniel's mother. Whether he is justified in this denial of paternity cannot be established, for the reader, like the narrator,[7] is never privy to any objective rendering of the facts. But what does emerge clearly is the fact that Daniel plays upon this doubt in order to furnish his own pockets:

"... I remember it like yesterday the morning he put a curse on me. Sixteen years old I was and anxious. I start very early. I walk all the way to Coulibri – five six hours it take. He don't refuse to see me; he receive me very cool and calm and first thing he tell me is I'm always pestering him for money. This because sometime I ask help to buy a pair of shoes and such. Not to go barefoot like a nigger. Which I am not. He look at me like I was dirt and I get angry too. 'I have my rights after all,' I tell him and you know what he do? He laugh in my face. When he finished laughing he call me what's-your-name. 'I can't remember all their names – it's too much to expect of me,' he says, talking to himself. Very old he look in the bright sunshine that morning. 'It's you yourself call me Daniel,' I tell him. 'I'm no slave like my mother was.'

" 'Your mother was a sly-boots if ever there was one,' he says, 'and I'm not a fool. However, the woman's dead and that's enough. But if there's one drop of my blood in your spindly carcass I'll eat my hat.' By this time my own blood at boiling point, I tell you, so I bawl back at him, 'Eat it then. Eat it. You haven't much time. Not much time either to kiss and love your new wife. She too young for you.' 'Great God!' he said and his face go red and then a kind of grey colour. He try to get up but he falls back in his chair. He have a big silver inkstand on his desk, and he throw it at my head and he curse me, but I duck and the inkstand hit the door. I have to laugh but I go off quick. He send me some money – not a word, only the money. It's the last time I see him." (pp.101–2)

The ambiguity of meaning within this passage is added to by the complexity of the narrative level which obtains here. This particular rendering appears to be a retrospective account in Daniel's own words. Its textual position, however, calls that status into question, for the entire rendering is contained within Edward's own retrospective narrative. The speech bears all the marks of being rendered word-for-word. This being so, it seems justifiable to assume that Edward has reconstituted the original utterance for the purposes of dramatic effect within his own narrative. There is a definite textual clue which demonstrates that these words are not rendered verbatim. The lack of any grammatical correspondence between the pidgin English attributed to Daniel, and the correct English which is supposed to have come from Antoinette's father, gives away this fact of reconstitution. I have no doubt that in the original utterance Daniel's rendering of Cosway's words would not have been exact, they would have been subjected to some grammatical transformation in line with the speaker's own poor grasp of the English language.

By contrast with the formality of this reconstitution, an impressionistic mode is adopted towards the end of Edward's narrative when the flux of his own consciousness is rendered. This is an important section,[8] for within it lies evidence of Edward's conception of himself as a tragic hero. In this respect, Edward's attitude to himself complements Daniel's efforts to project an image of himself as malcontent. We have already seen through Daniel; Edward's narrative rendering of him ensured that we would do so. With Edward, however, the lack of any subordination in terms of narrative level demands that if any puncturing of this self-image is to occur it must be achieved within his own narrative language.

An impressionistic setting is created at the beginning of the passage. As economically as possible, Edward depicts his position

within the natural landscape; he has retreated from human contact:

> Under the oleanders ... I watched the hidden mountains and
> the mists drawn over their faces. It's cool today; cool, calm and
> cloudy as an English summer. But a lovely place in any weather,
> however far I travel I'll never see a lovelier. (p.135)

It is significant that he should be alone. His thoughts are therefore
able to function as a soliloquy, in line with the approach in classical
tragedy. The poetic tone of his words is appreciated at once, and,
like that in blank verse, it intensifies the mood. His choice of the
epithet 'hidden' to describe the mountains recalls his earlier desire
for 'what it hides'.[9] This reminds us of his ambivalent feelings
towards nature which now contrast with his present attitude of
acceptance and appreciation. The lovely image of the mist which
acts as a veil to conceal the 'faces' of the mountains, is of
subconscious significance. It suggests a link with a young bride
whose beauty is concealed by her head-dress, and who remains
'untouched' until such time as that veil is removed. Thus, there is a
subliminal poignancy in the figure, for Edward's own conception
of his bride's sexual purity has, by now, been tainted. Consciously,
he bends the beauty of the scene to harmonise with an idea which
is far removed from the tropics – 'an English summer'. The
alliteration in 'cool, calm and cloudy', though rhythmically effective, does betray the mental effort to focus his thoughts away from
disturbing parallels. But, for the reader, the parallels remain, and
the textual juxtaposition of this passage with the previous one, in
which Edward was shown to be arranging Antoinette's incarceration, bestows a piquancy on his assertion that he will 'never see a
lovelier'.

The temporal perspective of this first paragraph is difficult to
determine. Owing to the interruption by ellipsis marks, the initial
phrase, 'Under the oleanders', is not distinctly located in time. It is
not absolutely clear whether the statement 'I watched' belongs
syntactically to that phrase since we cannot determine how much
of the intervening discourse has been omitted from the text.
Similarly, the impressionistic economy which allows Edward's
thoughts about the coolness and the loveliness of the place to be
rendered without any declarative verb, adds to this indeterminacy.
In the second paragraph, the declarative verb 'I thought' places the

thoughts on a retrospective level. The thoughts themselves, however, maintain the immediacy of the present tense, and thus the reader retains the impression of having direct access to them:

The hurricane months are not so far away, I thought, and saw that tree strike its roots deeper, making ready to fight the wind. Useless. If and when it comes they'll all go. Some of the royal palms stand (she told me). Stripped of their branches, tall like brown pillars, still they stand – defiant. Not for nothing are they called royal. The bamboos take an easier way, they bend to the earth and lie there, creaking, groaning, crying for mercy. The contemptuous wind passes, not caring for these abject things. (Let them live.) Howling, shrieking, laughing the wild blast passes.

Despite the seeming clarity which is brought to this paragraph by the declarative verb, the ambiguity of the temporal perspective is played upon still further. This occurs to such an extent that it gives rise to an extreme form of anachrony which manages to subvert the orientation totally. In this way, even the apparent retrospection of the stance is called into question. The ambiguity rests on the temporal status of the hurricane which is the subject of the paragraph. Initially, Edward suggests that the high winds have not yet occurred although they may be imminent. This uncertain state gives rise to a tension between the retrospective nature of his thoughts and the anticipatory nature of the projected weather conditions. With an alteration of main tense from the past to the present comes a lessening of that particular tension. Now, however, another past tense declarative verb, 'she told me', is subordinated within brackets, and subsequent to this sentence it is not clear whose consciousness is being rendered. We assume that the 'she' refers to Antoinette. Are we to understand that the remaining sentences in the paragraph, which all conform to the present tense, are words which she has also uttered? But the imagery in these lines – the 'defiant' palms, the 'contemptuous' wind, and the 'abject' attitude of the bamboos – closely harmonises with Edward's own imaginative assertion that the tree prepares to 'fight the wind'. Surely these lines belong to Edward himself.

The use of the present tense here suggests that a perfect temporal correspondence exists between what is being described – the raging wind – and the process of the description – Edward's act of narration. Thus, the status of the hurricane has undergone a radical alteration within this paragraph alone. However, as if that were not enough, at the beginning of the next paragraph the temporal logic of the discourse is again subverted when the following assertion is made – 'all that's some months away'. This qualification obscures the temporality of the preceding description of the storm, identifying it either as proleptic, if it is some months away in the future, or as analeptic, if it has already occurred:

> But all that's some months away. It's an English summer now, so cool, so grey. Yet I think of my revenge and hurricanes. Words rush through my head (deeds too). Words. Pity is one of them. It gives no rest.

His awareness of the concept of a tragic hero begins to be suggested with more force here. The idea of 'revenge' fits the classical pattern, while 'pity' is a component part of the Aristotelian cathartic effect experienced by the audience of a tragedy. Edward's lack of passion, however, deprives him of the stature of the genuine tragic hero. His idea of 'revenge' is linked to his idea of 'hurricanes', and we have already seen the insubstantiality of those within the play of his narrative. And Edward himself appears only subconsciously to be aware of his own shortcomings. His mention of 'deeds' suggests that they remain abstract, that they are conceptualised in his 'head' rather than actualised. Similarly, the 'pity' which he speaks of, and which he hopes the receivers of his narrative will feel for him, can never transcend the status of 'words'. Indeed, this is demonstrated in his text by the game of word association which he subsequently plays when 'pity' stimulates the memory of a line from *Macbeth*: 'pity, like a naked new-born babe,/ Striding the blast.'[10] The choice of quotation, a line uttered by one of Shakespeare's tragic heroes, does much to bolster Edward's idea of himself. And yet, the subsequent decline of his own words into bitterness and self-pity demonstrates, by implied contrast, the chasm which exists between the nobility of the classical tragic figure, and Edward himself:

> I read that long ago when I was young – I hate poets now and poetry. As I hate music which I loved once. Sing your songs Rupert the Rhine, but I'll not listen, though they tell me you've a sweet voice. . . .

Pity. Is there none for me? Tied to a lunatic for life – a drunken lying lunatic – gone her mother's way.

Given the poetic tone of his earlier words, his declared hatred of poetry here must be viewed ironically, and appreciated more as a tendency towards histrionics which, by its very nature, debars him from the desired status of tragic hero. His concern about the question of pity, too, demonstrates a consciousness of image which is not in keeping with the classical model. Where it applies in the case of the tragic hero, pity is evoked by the text; it is an emotion which the reader experiences owing to the nature of the drama and the characters concerned.

The dramatic intensity of the passage increases with the introduction into the text of Edward's memory of Christophine's words. The words are rendered directly, and this allows a dialectic to ensue as Edward responds to them:

> *"She love you so much, so much. She thirsty for you. Love her a little like she say. It's all that you can love – a little."*
> Sneer to the last, Devil. Do you think that I don't know? She thirsts for *anyone* – not for me ...
> She'll loosen her black hair, and laugh and coax and flatter (a mad girl. She'll not care who she's loving.) She'll moan and cry and give herself as no sane woman would – or could. *Or could.* Then lie so still, still as this cloudy day. A lunatic who always knows the time. But never does.
> Till she's drunk so deep, played her game so often that the lowest shrug and jeer at her. And I'm to know it – I? No. I've a trick worth two of that.
> *"She love you so much, so much. Try her once more."*
> I tell you she loves no one, anyone. I could not touch her. Excepting as the hurricane will touch that tree – and break it. You say I did? No. That was love's fierce play. Now I'll do it.
> (pp.135–6)

This extract provides us with categorical evidence of Edward's acts of reconstitution where the rendering of the words of other characters in his narrative is concerned. In effect, it modifies our conception of his reliability as narrator. If we compare the first of the two italicised utterances with its counterpart in Edward's original rendering of the scene between himself and Christophine, we will see that the earlier version differs from the one above:

> "... She love you so much. She thirsty for you. Wait, and perhaps you can love her again. A little, like she say. A little. Like you can love." (p.129)

Clearly, there is a great difference between the implications involved in each rendering of the final statement: 'A little. Like you can love.', and 'It's all that you can love – a little.' Of course, owing to the unreliability of the narrator, it is impossible to establish which of these two utterances is closer to Christophine's actual words as she uttered them in the diegesis. There are three reasons why it is likely that the former is a truer representation of them. Firstly, from a temporal point of view, its occurrence in the text is less distant from its occurrence in the actual diegesis. In this respect, we may assume that Edward would have been able to remember her words better on the first occasion of his rendering of them, because the time which had elapsed between their actual utterance and his narrating act would have been relatively less than that which would have elapsed between their utterance and his repeated rendering of them. Secondly, the unpolished, rather clipped grammatical structure of the former statement contrasts with the more fluent and bookish quality of the latter. In this respect, the latter speech pattern is more characteristic of Edward than of Christophine. Finally, it is important to take into account Edward's distressed state of mind in this second rendering of the words, and the effect which it would have on his memory. Since Christophine originally uttered them, he will have had time to dwell upon their implications – implications which are either real or imagined. Not being privy either to the actual utterance, or to the tone in which the words were uttered, the reader will never know whether Edward's interpretation of them is justified. Could it, like much else in his text, be a re-working of the facts for narrative effect? Certainly, the second version of these words provides the 'sneer' which Edward takes up in his dramatic challenge to the 'Devil'. That 'sneer' is not inherent in the original version as it stands, although such an attitude may have been intimated by Christophine in her vocal expression.

Again, the reiteration of Christophine's declaration that Antoinette 'loves' Edward comes in a different form from that in the first rendering. The statement *'She love you so much, so much. Try her once more.'* finds no exact counterpart in the earlier discourse. Instead, the exhortation to 'Try her once more' is there bound up with the notion of Antoinette's vulnerability should she be forsaken by Edward:

> ". . . She don't satisfy you? Try her once more, I think she satisfy you now. If you forsake her they will tear her in pieces – like they did her mother." (p.130)

By abstracting certain words, and ignoring the particular context in which they were originally uttered, Edward demonstrates the sheer cruelty of his proposed action. It would not be appropriate for him in this bitter mood of self-pity to allow the focus to fall on the idea of Antoinette as victim. And yet, the reader remembers the context in which her words were originally uttered, as well as the purpose of Christophine's selfless advice. Edward's own egotism contrasts with our memory of the fidelity and love of Antoinette's black servant. The echo of her words, despite their partial reconstitution, keeps our memory of her in our minds, and this, as well as the subject of her concern – Antoinette's own mental frailty – serves to intensify our recognition of Edward's decline into abject self-absorption:

> She'll not laugh in the sun again. She'll not dress up and smile at herself in that damnable looking-glass. So pleased, so satisfied.
> Vain, silly creature. Made for loving? Yes, but she'll have no lover, for I don't want her and she'll see no other. (p.136)

This, then, is Edward's 'revenge'. Ironically, his own choice of words punctures his pretension towards the status of tragic hero. It is the belittling description of Antoinette as a 'vain, silly creature' which does the most damage to his own self-image. This description, once uttered, places his proposed actions towards her on a level far baser than that we associate with the nobility of the classical hero. His projected incarceration of her appears peevish and spiteful rather than justified by any lofty notions of 'revenge'. Certainly, there is a tragedy within this account, but it is connected with Antoinette's own fate, with her powerlessness to avert the suffocation of spirit which is in store for her. And, on a subliminal level, Edward appears to recognise this:

The tree shivers. Shivers and gathers all its strength. And waits.

(There is a cool wind blowing now – a cold wind. Does it carry the babe born to the blast of hurricanes?)

Here, the intensity of our sympathy for Antoinette is augmented by the sheer poetry of Edward's utterance. The effect is most unusual. The poetry appears to be working against Edward, and yet it springs from a source which lies deep within him. Perhaps we have at last come upon the root of his own tragedy. His conscious hatred of poetry would, if it were allowed to gain control of him, deny expression to this spiritual impulse. But, as we see, the impulse is too strong to be suppressed. It is, I think, at this point that we feel most pity for Edward, whose natural inclinations have been perverted by influences which are external to him. In this respect, we may view him as a man who acts against his own nature:

> She said she loved this place. This is the last she'll see of it. I'll watch for one tear, one human tear. Not that blank hating moonstruck face. I'll listen. . . . If she says good-bye perhaps adieu. *Adieu* – like those old-time songs she sang. Always *adieu* (and all songs say it). If she too says it, or weeps, I'll take her in my arms, my lunatic. She's mad but *mine, mine*. What will I care for gods or devils or for Fate itself. If she smiles or weeps or both. *For me.*
>
> Antoinetta – I can be gentle too. Hide your face. Hide yourself but in my arms. You'll soon see how gentle. My lunatic. My mad girl.
>
> Here's a cloudy day to help you. No brazen sun.
>
> No sun . . . No sun. The weather's changed.

In opposition to our feelings for Edward, which have been evoked in spite of his earlier melodramatic pursuit of them, these lines fill us with dread. We shrink from this extremity of possessiveness, fearing the devastating effect which it will inevitably have on Antoinette. The final lines are of ominous significance. We recall that the name 'Antoinetta' rhymes with 'marionetta', and the idea of Antoinette as a doll, having no control over her own destiny, is re-evoked. The change in the weather presages the colder climate of England where she will finally be deprived of both her liberty and her natural environment. And yet, despite the portentousness of the language, and our own awareness of the grim fate which awaits Antoinette, we are able to anticipate the outcome with a calmness which must be born of a cathartic effect engendered by those opposed emotions of pity and fear. This is the essence of the tragic effect, and it is achieved brilliantly under the guise of a deliberate effort to subvert it.

The sense of inevitability about Antoinette's fate, which accounts, in part, for the equanimity with which we face the final débâcle, has been prepared for early on and throughout the development of the text. Instrumental in its evocation has been the device of the dream sequence. On three separate occasions, the contents of a particularly 'bad dream' which Antoinette repeatedly experiences, are rendered in the discourse. With each successive rendering more details emerge, so that a disturbing picture of the dream in its entirety is gradually built up.

The text demonstrates that Antoinette has been plagued with this dream ever since she was a child. She first experiences it on the evening of the day on which she argues with Tia. On this occasion, she cannot understand the details, but the distressing emotion of fear is evoked within her:

> I went to bed early and slept at once. I dreamed that I was walking in the forest. Not alone. Someone who hated me was with me, out of sight. I could hear heavy footsteps coming closer and though I struggled and screamed I could not move. I woke crying. The covering sheet was on the floor and my mother was looking down at me. (p.23)

Here, the retrospective tense which is employed in the rendering serves to keep the content of the dream at a controlled distance. On the second occasion of its rendering, however, an alteration to the present tense effects a lessening of that distance between the experience and the narrative act, thus making the rendering all the more immediate and dramatically effective. This time the dream occurs during Antoinette's period of adolescence, after she has lost her mother, and while she is staying at the convent:

> This was the second time I had my dream.
> Again I have left the house at Coulibri. It is still night and I am walking towards the forest. I am wearing a long dress and thin

slippers, so I walk with difficulty, following the man who is with me and holding up the skirt of my dress. It is white and beautiful and I don't wish to get it soiled. I follow him, sick with fear but I make no effort to save myself; if anyone were to try to save me, I would refuse. This must happen. Now we have reached the forest. We are under the tall dark trees and there is no wind. "Here?" He turns and looks at me, his face black with hatred, and when I see this I begin to cry. He smiles slyly. "Not here, not yet," he says, and I follow him, weeping. Now I do not try to hold up my dress, it trails in the dirt, my beautiful dress. We are no longer in the forest but in an enclosed garden surrounded by a stone wall and the trees are different trees. I do not know them. There are steps leading upwards. It is too dark to see the wall or the steps, but I know they are there and I think, "It will be when I go up these steps. At the top." I stumble over my dress and cannot get up. I touch a tree and my arms hold on to it. "Here, here." But I think I will not go any further. The tree sways and jerks as if it is trying to throw me off. Still I cling and the seconds pass and each one is a thousand years. "Here, in here," a strange voice said, and the tree stopped swaying and jerking. (p.50)

The content of the dream, rendered in the present, is framed within two short sentences which are governed by the perfect tense – 'This was the second time I had my dream. Again I have left the house at Coulibri', and '"Here, in here," a strange voice said, and the tree stopped swaying and jerking.' The substance of the final sentence may be shown to connect both with the dream, being a reiteration of the man's earlier command to Antoinette, and, by its return to the main tense of the first narrative, with the subsequent reality when the Sister leads her from the dormitory into another room. Within this framework, the dream itself is allowed to unfold in an apparently simultaneous narrative form, although we know that this form has been adopted by the narrator, the majority of whose text is otherwise rendered from a retrospective point of view. In introducing the context, the narrator maintains the perfect mode. The repeated status of the dream is immediately focused upon with the word 'Again'. Now, though, Antoinette's new geographical location is implied in the reference to 'the house at Coulibri'. When last she experienced the dream, this detail was already understood, since she was living there at the time. This then, is an important development in the dream sequence. On each successive occurrence she experiences it in a different place.

With the onset of the present tense, the action gets under way, and it is when Antoinette is depicted 'walking towards the forest' that we recognise both the similarity and the difference between the content of this and the previous rendering. 'The forest' is the common signifier by which we can identify the same location. In this version, however, detail which occurs prior to the starting point of the initial account is included. There, we were not informed of anything that occurred before Antoinette was actually in the forest. Here, too, the previously suppressed details of Antoinette's clothing emerge, and this is another important development. If we take into consideration the fact that this second experience of the dream occurs during a period of adolescence, we may find some subliminal sexual significance in the description of the clothes. Firstly, the 'long dress' prepares us for the idea of wedding attire, and this is reinforced by the 'thin slippers'. On occasions such as marriage, the physical adornment of women is regarded as more important than their own comfort. It is not surprising, therefore, that Antoinette finds her freedom of movement restricted – 'I walk with difficulty'. But, more importantly, the colour 'white' suggests purity, and is associated with the traditional colour of bridal gowns. Her assertion that the dress is not only 'white' but 'beautiful' too, lends more weight to the idea that she is clothed for marriage. The dress itself soon acts as a signifier for her own sexual purity. Her disinclination to get it 'soiled', coupled with her emotion 'sick with fear', suggests the sort of trepidation with which a young girl might face the loss of her virginity. And yet, despite the fear, she stresses her recognition of the inevitability of what must occur: '. . . but I make no effort to save myself; if anyone were to try to save me, I would refuse. This must happen,' It is this sense of inevitability which emphasises the terrifying nature of Antoinette's experience in the dream. The sexual significance of the content which, as I have shown, is brought out through implication rather than direct statement, is the key to understanding this fear. And, in this respect, Antoinette's fear must be augmented by the shadowy identity of 'the man' who accompanies her. We recall that in the first version the portrait of this character was even more vague than it is here. There, even his sex was not determined, he was merely 'someone'. Now, however, the emergence of his maleness has a definite part to play in the implied sexual significance of the whole.

At last, we come to the point in the diegesis of the dream with which the first version of it had begun – 'Now we have reached the forest.' Here, too, more details emerge, this time concerned with the forest itself, and these, in turn, contribute to the atmosphere of fearfulness which is evoked in the entire scene: 'We are under the tall dark trees and there is no wind.' Within this setting, more physical details of the man also emerge, and they too add to the sense of hostility – his face is 'black with hatred', and when he smiles he does so 'slyly'. By this time, the 'weeping' Antoinette has resigned herself to the idea of her fate. She no longer attempts to protect the whiteness of her dress, allowing it, rather, to trail 'in the dirt'. Here a temporal ellipsis occurs in the text, which is not indicated by punctuation marks but by a sudden change of location. This is quite consistent with the perverse logic of dreams: 'We are no longer in the forest but in an enclosed garden surrounded by a stone wall and the trees are different trees.' The garden itself is not identified; clearly, it is not that of Coulibri Estate which Antoinette knows intimately, and which she would un-doubtedly recognise. Her lack of familiarity with the surroundings is, in fact, emphasised by her inability to recognise the trees. There is ambivalence in her assertion that she does not 'know them'. This could refer either to the actual trees, implying that she has never seen these particular ones before, or it could suggest that she is unfamiliar with that type of tree. If the second sense were to prevail, it must imply that the location has altered to a totally different geographical region, in which the flora is of a species which is new to her. Could these be the 'English trees' (p.135) which Edward himself, in a later passage, yearns to see? If so, it would seem likely that the description presages Antoinette's removal to the enclave of Thornfield Hall. Certainly, the 'enclosed' situation of the garden, suggesting no means of escape, would conform with the idea of her imprisonment. The 'steps leading upwards', and the significance of being 'at the top' of them, also seem to point to a position which is in harmony with that of the attic room in which she is finally incarcerated. And the darkness which obscures her vision of both 'the wall' and 'the steps' emphasises that her sense of her own restriction is an intuitive one – 'I know they are there'. For the reader, this in itself must add to the horror of her experience. Were the wall and the steps actual objects, she might, perhaps, overcome them. But when the imprisonment is as much mental as physical, then there is no easy means of escape from it.

The position 'at the top', which is of such importance in Antoinette's understanding of the situation, could, as I have said, point to the attic room. On the other hand, on a second reading, we will recall that her final triumph over her imprisonment at Thornfield Hall occurs when she burns the house down and leaps to her own death from the battlements, at the same time achieving a release from her mental chains. Read in the light of this particular ending, the final part of the passage may be shown to presage the very débâcle of the text. In the respect of this, apart from the ambivalent notion of 'the top', the narrowing of focus from 'trees' in general, to one particular tree, is of great significance. Initially, the function of the tree is one of support – 'my arms hold on to it'. We are inclined to relate this tree to that other upon which particular focus had fallen earlier – 'the tree of life' (p.16). This idea is reinforced when the tree in question 'sways and jerks' despite the lack of wind which has already been carefully pointed out. Antoinette's conviction that its intention is to 'throw' her off leads to a most revealing response – 'I cling'. The word 'cling' occurs on only one other occasion in the entire text, and then it is used with a distinct reference to life: 'The first day I had to go to the convent, I clung to Aunt Cora as you would cling to life if you loved it.' (p.41). An understanding of the metaphorical dimension of this signifier 'tree' is necessary if we are to connect the content of the dream with Antoinette's fall to her death from the rooftops of Thornfield Hall. For the moment, however, the dream is not allowed to end, the tree does not succeed in throwing her off. Instead, the mysterious destination which is indicated by the signifier 'here', is reached, although the abrupt ending of the dream suspends the unfolding of that particular mystery. The 'strange voice' points to a new persona, someone other than 'the man' whose voice has been heard by now, and who is, therefore, no longer 'strange'. This is where reality merges with the dream, prior to Antoinette's return to wakefulness.

The full significance of the dream remains suspended until the final pages of the text when a retrospective rendering of its third occurrence supplies an ending for it. This time, Antoinette makes no attempt to evoke the drama of the dream through the adoption of a simultaneous narrative approach. Instead, the drama of the experience is appreciated in her growing understanding of its significance. As we see her reconstructing the details in her mind, so we see that mind grappling with the hidden meaning of the dream, and moving towards what the reader appreciates as a most terrifying conclusion.

The tension begins, however, in a paragraph which occurs immediately prior to Antoinette's rendering of the dream. She has just learned of her attack on Richard Mason who had visited her on the previous evening. In the twisted logic of her mind, she is convinced that she would not have attacked him had he recognised her, and that his recognition of her depended upon her wearing of her red dress. We recall that this is the dress which she had worn on the occasion of her last meeting with her lover, Sandi Cosway, and thus it has a particular significance for her. But if we are to believe Antoinette's account, this is also the dress which Edward, 'that man', disapproves of, for he claims that it makes her look 'intemperate and unchaste' (p.152). This remark is quite characteristic of Edward, for subconsciously he would register that the colour red is identified with passion, and passion, as we know, is an anathema to him, especially when it is seen as an attribute of his wife. But the colour red is also symbolically linked with fire, and Antoinette registers this connection on a subliminal level. The two ideas are bonded in her choice of figurative language with which she describes the dress:

> But I looked at the dress on the floor and it was as if the fire had spread across the room. It was beautiful and it reminded me of something I must do. I will remember I thought. I will remember quite soon now. (p.153)

Her subsequent rendering of the dream is, therefore, received by the reader in this context of Antoinette searching for a course of action, and it is this which adds to the tension of the final pages. Her violent behaviour towards Richard Mason, coupled with our recognition of her attraction towards fire, implies that any course of action which she chooses is likely to be quite explosive. Thanks to the presence of Grace Poole in this section, by now the link with *Jane Eyre* is unmistakable, and our knowledge of the ending of that novel adds to the sense of inevitability about the path which Antoinette will take.

Between the above paragraph and the rendering of the dream, there is an ellipsis of an indefinite duration. It is in this textual lacuna that the third occurrence of the dream actually takes place:

> That was the third time I had my dream, and it ended. I know now that the flight of steps leads to this room where I lie watching the woman asleep with her head on her arms. In my dream I waited until she began to snore, then I got up, took the keys and let myself out with a candle in my hand. It was easier this time than ever before and I walked as though I were flying.

Antoinette's immediate assertion that the dream 'ended' places our appreciation of her rendering of it in a unique position. We now view the ensuing discourse as emanating from a mind which has more than a mere partial understanding of the story she tells. The present tense stance which she had adopted for the rendering of its second occurrence now seems to have been even more significant than we initially took it for. There, she did not know the ending of the dream, and consequently, her understanding of it was limited. The implied simultaneity between the actual experience and the narrating act emphasised this lack of ultimate knowledge. Now, however, she writes from the point of view of one who knows how the story will end. Her choice of a retrospective stance clarifies the distinction between this rendering and the previous one. And immediately, too, she reinforces the idea of her greater knowledge when she writes 'I know now . . .'. But her knowledge, though greater than it was previously, is not complete:

> All the people who had been staying in the house had gone, for the bedroom doors were shut, but it seemed to me that someone was following me, someone was chasing me, laughing. Sometimes I looked to the right or to the left but I never looked behind me for I did not want to see that ghost of a woman whom they say haunts this place. I went down the staircase. I went further than I had ever been before. There was someone talking in one of the rooms. I passed it without noise, slowly.

In common with the first version, although not with the second, Antoinette senses that she is being followed by a person who is not distinguished – 'someone'. This time, however, she does not sense hatred in her pursuer. Her knowledge of the myth of the ghost of Thornfield Hall, acquired during a previous excursion into the main part of the house, is used by her, subconsciously, to account

for her sense of a presence. Her failure to connect this reputed
spectre with herself is a clear sign of her lack of ultimate knowledge. The reader, however, knowing the story of *Jane Eyre*,
appreciates the dramatic irony in her own description of her
movements – 'without noise, slowly' – which typifies the received
idea of ghostliness.

> At last I was in the hall where a lamp was burning. I remember
> that when I came. A lamp and the dark staircase and the veil
> over my face. They think I don't remember but I do. There was a
> door to the right. I opened it and went in. It was a large room
> with a red carpet and red curtains. Everything else was white. I
> sat down on a couch to look at it and it seemed sad and cold and
> empty to me, like a church without an altar. I wished to see it
> clearly so I lit all the candles, and there were many. I lit them
> carefully from the one I was carrying but I couldn't reach up to
> the chandelier. Then I looked round for the altar for with so
> many candles and so much red, the room reminded me of a
> church. Then I heard a clock ticking and it was made of gold.
> Gold is the idol they worship. (pp.153–4)

The retrospective mode which is adopted for this rendering of the
dream is not distinguishable from the main tense of the first
narrative. Consequently, some ambiguity may arise when
Antoinette momentarily shifts the level back to that of the first
narrative, as she does in this paragraph. The shift occurs with the
assertion that she remembers part of the house from the time that
she saw it on her arrival there. When she returns to the analeptic
level of the dream with 'There was a door to the right', there is no
means of telling immediately that this is again part of the dream. A
blurring of distinction between dream and reality has been
effected, and the textual approach reflects Antoinette's own confusion between the two states.

Through the colour red and the ticking clock, the appearance of
the room is reminiscent of that of Daniel Cosway. Antoinette's
assertion that 'Gold is the idol they worship' is important in this
respect, for in making it, she unconsciously draws a parallel
between that grasping character and Rochester himself, who owns
the room which she describes. A further parallel between the two
men emerges implicitly in her use of religious imagery, by which
she draws a comparison between this room and a Protestant

church. We have already discussed the influence of religion in Daniel Cosway's life. His role as a 'preacher' identifies him as a member of the Protestant rather than the Catholic Church. Now, Edward's Protestant background is brought out by Antoinette, who sees it reflected in the atmosphere of the place. And it is this use of imagery which demonstrates another fundamental dissimilarity between herself and her husband. In her reference to 'a church without an altar', which, to her, makes for a 'sad and cold and empty' place, she reveals her own natural disinclination for the simplicity of such a denomination. No doubt, her Catholic upbringing has imbued her with a love of altars and candles, and it is this atmosphere which she attempts to re-create in the room.

A sudden change of mood may be accounted for by the failure of her act of re-creation to transport her back to the Catholic period of her life – her childhood and adolescence – when she had felt comparatively safe. Possibly, it is her consciousness of the materialism of these people too, which brings her back to the reality of her present position:

> Suddenly I felt very miserable in that room, though the couch I was sitting on was so soft that I sank into it. It seemed to me that I was going to sleep. Then I imagined that I heard a footstep and I thought what will they say, what will they do if they find me here? I held my right wrist with my left hand and waited. But it was nothing. I was very tired after this. Very tired. I wanted to get out of the room but my own candle had burned down and I took one of the others. (p.154)

There is pathos in the detail of the softness of the couch. Clearly, Antoinette is not used to such comfort in the spartan conditions of the attic rooms where she is confined. This is a subtle touch by Rhys through which the cruelty of Rochester is implied. And there are other signs in this passage which keep him in our minds. Antoinette's fear of being found reinforces the idea of the injustice of her treatment. Her physical stance too, holding her right wrist with her left hand, is designed to remind us of Rochester, for we recall that he is annoyed by this habit of hers. Possibly her desire to 'get out of the room' reflects a desire to be free of all the restrictions imposed on her by him.

For a moment, Antoinette does achieve liberation from her situation when, in a dream-within-a-dream, she is transported

back to the West Indies; but the moment does not last, and her
focus soon returns to Thornfield Hall:

> Suddenly I was in Aunt Cora's room. I saw the sunlight coming
> through the window, the tree outside and the shadows of the
> leaves on the floor, but I saw the wax candles too and I hated
> them. So I knocked them all down. Most of them went out but
> one caught the thin curtains that were behind the red ones. I
> laughed when I saw the lovely colour spreading so fast, but I did
> not stay to watch it. I went into the hall again with the tall candle
> in my hand. It was then that I saw her – the ghost. The woman
> with streaming hair. She was surrounded by a gilt frame but I
> knew her. I dropped the candle I was carrying and it caught the
> end of a tablecloth and I saw flames shoot up. As I ran or
> perhaps floated or flew I called help me Christophine help me
> and looking behind me I saw that I had been helped. There was a
> wall of fire protecting me but it was too hot, it scorched me and I
> went away from it.

Her flight to 'Aunt Cora's room' is significant. We remember that it
was Aunt Cora who, as well as Christophine, filled a maternal role
in Antoinette's life, loving and caring for her as she would have
done had she been the girl's real mother. But the image of Aunt
Cora is not strong enough to efface that symbolised by the 'wax
candles'. Antoinette's return to the room in Thornfield Hall is a
reluctant one, and this negative attitude is suggested by her
new-found hatred of the candles. Ironically, her violent response
towards them has an effect in which she delights, not recognising
the danger to herself which the fire threatens. Indeed, in her state
of mental distraction, she avoids a direct reference to the consequence of her violence, even substituting for the noun 'fire' the
metaphor 'lovely colour'. A measure of her abstractedness may be
seen in her failure to recognise herself in the mirror which she
finds in the hall. The 'gilt frame' which surrounds the image of
'The woman with the streaming hair' signifies that the image itself
is, in fact, a reflection of Antoinette. Antoinette takes what she sees
there to be the 'ghost', and in this she is not far wrong. Certainly,
the myth of the ghost has arisen from various sightings of
Antoinette herself wandering around the main part of the house.
Her earlier awareness of being followed was, in fact, a sensitivity to
her own shadow, hence the lack of hostility in the atmosphere

which prevailed at the time. But this failure to recognise herself in the mirror is the mark of a complete breakdown in her recognition of her own identity. And the disorientation which it implies finds a parallel in her uncertainty about her own movement – 'As I ran or perhaps floated or flew . . .'. In such a state, it is not surprising that she calls for the assistance of the only other mother-figure of her experience – Christophine. Her disorientation and uncertainty about her sense of self is reflected textually too, in the merging of her direct speech into the matrix of the narrative, with no distinguishing features of quotation marks to indicate its separateness: '. . . I called help me Christophine help me and looking behind me I saw that I had been helped.' This is a disturbing sign, but perhaps even more disturbing is the reassertion of her inability to recognise the danger of the fire, and, indeed, her misconception of its purpose: 'There was a wall of fire protecting me but it was too hot, it scorched me and I went away from it.' Her response to the heat is determined purely through the senses, and not by any rational appreciation of its danger.

Her movement away from the fire is important if the details of the dream are to develop. We recall that on the previous rendering she sensed the significance of mounting the stairs, and our memory of her words, 'It will be when I go up these steps. At the top.', haunts our present perception of her ascent:

> There were more candles on a table and I took one of them and ran up the first flight of stairs and the second. On the second floor I threw away the candle. But I did not stay to watch. I ran up the last flight of stairs and along the passage. I passed the room where they brought me yesterday or the day before yesterday, I don't remember. Perhaps it was quite long ago for I seemed to know the house quite well. I knew how to get away from the heat and the shouting, for there was shouting now. When I was out on the battlements it was cool and I could hardly hear them. I sat there quietly. I don't know how long I sat. Then I turned round and saw the sky. It was red and all my life was in it. (pp.154–5)

The significance of her climbing of the stairs may be seen in her slowing up of the pace of the narrative so that her negotiation of each particular flight is noted in the account. A sense of urgency about her movement, her desire to reach the top, may be detected

in her attitude to the candle which she threw away – 'I did not stay
to watch'. These words also indicate the drama which she initiates
but which remains within a part of the diegesis at one remove from
the text. A little later, the detail of the 'shouting' will add to our
sense of this activity which occurs simultaneously to the time of
our own narrative but to which we have no other access than the
implications of certain words and phrases in Antoinette's report.
But our awareness of the fire beneath her is important, for it creates
a tension as we realise that, once out on the battlements, any path
to safety is now blocked. She has effectively cut off her links with
the world downstairs, a world which she has always found
threatening, and now we begin to see the awful logic in her
recognition of the protective dimension of the fire.

Gradually, as the flames take hold, they are reflected in the night
sky, and it is at this point, the point almost of death, that
Antoinette's life flashes before her:

> I saw the grandfather clock and Aunt Cora's patchwork, all
> colours, I saw orchids and the stephanotis and the jasmine and
> the tree of life in flames. I saw the chandelier and the red carpet
> downstairs and the bamboos and the tree ferns, the gold ferns
> and the silver, and the soft green velvet of the moss on the
> garden wall. I saw my doll's house and the books and the picture
> of the Miller's Daughter. I heard the parrot call as he did when
> he saw a stranger, *Qui est là? Qui est là?* and the man who hated
> me was calling too, Bertha! Bertha! The wind caught my hair and
> it streamed out like wings. It might bear me up, I thought, if I
> jumped to those hard stones. But when I looked over the edge I
> saw the pool at Coulibri. Tia was there. She beckoned to me and
> when I hesitated she laughed. I heard her say, You frightened?
> And I heard the man's voice, Bertha! Bertha! All this I saw and
> heard in a fraction of a second. And the sky so red. Someone
> screamed and I thought, *Why did I scream?* I called 'Tia!' and
> jumped and woke. (p.155)

The heat and colour which she has introduced into her surroundings suggest that West Indian climate which she has missed in the
coldness of England. In this respect, her act of setting fire to
Thornfield Hall may be regarded as having been born of a creative
rather than a destructive impulse. Just as the phoenix is said to rise
from ashes, so her island home is evoked in her imagination
through the effect of the flames on the English sky. Her love of

colour, seen already in the metaphor which she substituted for 'fire', is seen here too in her detailing of 'all colours' – the 'red carpet', the 'gold ferns and the silver', the 'soft green' of the moss. The sheer profusion of the images is suggested by the repetition of 'and'. Technically, this has the effect of making the flow pulsate, so that each separate item is given due attention, appearing in the sentence in a space created especially for it, and syntactically separated from every other item by the rhythmical renewal of the conjunction rather than by a summarising device. Furthermore, the reiteration of the phrase 'I saw' lends a special cadence to the flow, adding to the antiphonal effect of the passage. This is a moment of pure poetry, a lyrical oasis in the intensity of the final pages. To be appreciated fully, it should be freed from its textual bonds by being read aloud.

From Antoinette's present perspective, there is much pathos as well as nostalgia in her view of certain childhood treasures. Her reference to her 'doll's house' fills us with pity for her lost innocence; her inclusion of the 'picture of the Miller's Daughter' too, reminds us of her eager desire for an English life-style. Both of these items, however, also serve to remind us of her husband's attitude to her. Firstly, we recall his reduction of her to the status of a doll with the play on her name, 'Antoinetta, Marionetta'. Secondly, there is the question of his inability to come to terms with her individuality born of a foreign nature; an English clone of the type suggested by the portrait of the Miller's Daughter would, no doubt, have suited him better. There is a further suggestion of male cruelty implied in the reference to the parrot whose wings had been clipped by Mr Mason, and when Antoinette applies the image of 'wings' to her own hair, she brings out the link between herself and this mutilated bird. Just as Coco, having been deprived of the power of flight, fell to his death from the railings of the glacis, so too, Antoinette's hair will fail to support her in her leap from the battlements of Thornfield Hall.

Consistent with the logic of dreams, the level of the narrative becomes quite complex in this part of the passage. The dream-within-a-dream device by which her youth has been evoked gives way to a blurring of the boundaries between the two different dreams, so that images from one of them merge with those from the other. In this way, within one sentence we move from a focus on the parrot's cry of 'Qui est là?' to that of Rochester himself, who calls for his wife – 'Bertha! Bertha!' This sentence reinforces our idea of the parallel between Antoinette and the bird, and a whole new angle of significance emerges from its structure. The sentence 'Qui est là?' means 'Who is it?', 'Who is there?' Edward's refusal to call Antoinette by her own Christian name is yet another challenge to her sense of her own identity. In her mind, there is much confusion on the subject of exactly who *is* there. We have already seen this with regard to her lack of recognition of her own mirror image. Here too, she does not immediately make a link between the person who screamed – 'someone' – and herself; 'Someone screamed and I thought, Why did I scream?' The juxtaposition of the two utterances, therefore, implies significance in the bird's speech which might otherwise never have emerged. Added to that, however, Tia's presence in the dream reinforces the question of Antoinette's confused sense of identity. The black girl's attitude is one of hostility, and this reminds us of her mood during a squabble over money, which had preceded the final rift between them. We recall that on the occasion of their last violent meeting, Antoinette was disturbed by a firm identification of herself with Tia: 'It was as if I saw myself. Like in a looking-glass.' (p.38). Thus, for her, Tia represents her alter-ego, an extension of herself, and the gesture of beckoning, together with Antoinette's jump, may therefore be seen as a positive act of establishing her own sense of self, of going forward to meet the identity which she has been deprived of in the unnatural environment imposed upon her. Part of the tragedy, of course, is that Antoinette does not recognise the death of the body which is a necessary corollary of what she must see as a leap to freedom.

The climax of the dream is interrupted by Antoinette's return to wakefulness. At this point, the focus returns to her hideous prison – the attic room at Thornfield Hall. The resumption of the discourse on the first narrative level can come as rather a shock. So detailed and developed is the dream, and so indistinct is the mode from that of the first narrative, that we might be forgiven for confusing the dream with the reality of the diegesis, and forgetting, for a moment, that Antoinette is safely in her bed. Logically, we should respond with relief on remembering that Antoinette has not, in fact, leapt to her death from the battlements. And yet, as we have seen, for Antoinette the experience of the dream is a positive one. Our own response is ambivalent. On the one hand, we cannot fail to have been moved by the lyrical heights to which her discourse attained, and yet, we are filled with fear for the violence of her end. The prospect of Antoinette having to endure life in the dismal surroundings of the attic room is a pitiful one, and, indeed, we realise that after the experience of the dream, it cannot, any longer, be regarded as a possibility by her:

> Grace Poole was sitting at the table but she had heard the scream too, for she said, "What was that?" She got up, came over and looked at me. I stayed still, breathing evenly with my eyes shut. "I must have been dreaming," she said. Then she went back, not to the table but to her bed. I waited a long time after I heard her snore, then I got up, took the keys and unlocked the door. I was outside holding my candle. Now at last I know why I was brought here and what I have to do. There must have been a draught for the flame flickered and I thought it was out. But I shielded it with my hand and it burned up again to light me along the dark passage. (pp.155–6)

The narrative jolt created through the phrase 'and woke', which shakes us out of our engagement with the dream and brings us back to a focus on the first narrative, finds a parallel within the diegesis itself in the experience of Grace Poole who awakens on hearing Antoinette's scream. Her words 'I must have been dreaming' are, therefore, full of dramatic irony. Antoinette's own return to wakefulness occurs simultaneously to that of Mrs Poole, and thus there is a complete harmonising of response, not only with the characters in the diegesis, but also between them and the reader. The harmony soon disappears, however, when Antoinette deliberately waits for Grace Poole to go back to the sleep which had momentarily been disturbed for her. When this happens, there is an alteration of tense to the present, which demonstrates Antoinette's movement away from the retrospective mode of the first narrative, and presages her removal both from the diegesis itself, and thus from the reader's attention. The sign is only momentary, lasting for no longer than one sentence: 'Now at last I know why I was brought here and what I have to do.' Its effect, however, is profound, filling us with a sense of fearful anticipation. We too, unlike Grace Poole, know what is in her mind. When the time comes, however, she must face the leap alone. Logically, the first-person point of view precludes our sharing of her final, tragic end – the text must be broken off before that point is reached. The suspension of the discourse at the moment when she sets off to fulfil the prophecy of the dream, however, makes for a most powerful conclusion to the novel.

Conclusion

In my introduction to this book, I indicated that a major concern of critical theorists today lies with the idea of reading as a process which creates the text. I also identified the need for a reader-based textual analysis of the work of Jean Rhys, an analysis which would liberate the novels from a forced relationship to the writer herself. My attempt to generate just such a reading of these texts has also been an attempt to compensate for the over-simplification of the 'Rhys woman'. By focusing on each main character in turn, I have tried to highlight her complexity as an individual personality rather than as a part of a synthesised whole. At the same time, however, I have not ignored the link of gender which connects all these women, and all other women too, who struggle to find their own form of authority in a patriarchal society.

My opening remarks called into question the validity of the label 'passive victim' where it is applied to Rhys's main characters. On the one hand, of course, it is fair to say that in the patriarchal society which is the setting for each of these novels, the role of the woman is to be passive. In this respect, the Rhys woman's lot does not differ from that of any woman immersed within the same oppressive system. On the other hand, however, the term ignores this very struggle for authority, 'struggle', by definition, being incompatible with the concept of 'passivity'. Where Rhys's heroines are concerned, the struggle concerns itself not with a physical grouping together in solidarity against the oppressive forces, but rather in the more subtle way of each becoming her own maker of fiction. As such, and as we have seen, the 'Rhys woman' has the power to build texts and to articulate her own narratives. In this respect, as the author of her own discourse, she sets herself against the suffocation of her spirit, a suffocation which the traditionally expected 'passivity' would surely bring her.

Where Marya was concerned, the inclination to articulate her own text was shown in the narrative orientation of the novel. Despite the use of the third-person mode, it was Marya's perspective, her own irony, which motivated the discourse. In *After Leaving Mr Mackenzie*, alternative viewpoints added to the difficulty of reading the main character, but they did not rob the discourse of Julia's particular narrative authority. The autodiegetic nature of the text in the remaining three novels seemed to be a logical technical development in Rhys's style. Both Anna and Sasha emerged openly as makers of their own texts, in full control of their discourses. Finally, because the autodiegetic platform in *Wide Sargasso Sea* was shared between two different people, it was necessary to analyse the voices both of Antoinette and Edward. Despite my stated intention to make the 'Rhys woman' the main object of my focus in this book, it was important for me to explore Edward's self-image, for I saw this as having a significant bearing on the plight of Antoinette, and I located within it a basis for the evocation of a tragic intensity in the novel as a whole.

Edward's authority in his text is matched by his diegetic authority. As a man, 'the important person', his power is supreme. Antoinette documents her own tragic escape from this suffocating power into madness. When the two texts are juxtaposed, as they are in this novel, Antoinette's story makes for a very powerful conclusion, a conclusion which has inescapable feminist significance in the work of a consciously non-feminist writer.

Notes

INTRODUCTION

1. Gérard Genette, *Figures of Literary Discourse* (Oxford: Blackwell, 1982) p.70.
2. Louis James, *Jean Rhys* (London: Longman, 1978); Thomas Staley, *Jean Rhys: A Critical Study* (London: Macmillan, 1979); Peter Wolfe, *Jean Rhys* (Boston: Twayne, 1980); Helen Nebeker, *Jean Rhys: Woman in Passage: A Critical Study of the Novels of Jean Rhys* (Montreal: Eden Press Women's Publications, 1981).
3. Staley, p.36.
4. Diana Trilling, 'The Odd Career of Jean Rhys', *The New York Times Book Review*, 25 May 1980, p.17.
5. Elgin Mellown, 'Character and Themes in the Novels of Jean Rhys', *Contemporary Literature*, 13, 1972, p.464.
6. Walter Allen, 'Bertha the Doomed', *The New York Times Book Review*, 18 June 1967, p.5.
7. Marcelle Bernstein, 'The Inscrutable Miss Jean Rhys', *Observer Magazine*, 1 June 1969, p.40.
8. Ned Thomas, 'Meeting Jean Rhys', *Planet*, 33, 1976, p.29.
9. Jean Rhys, 'Making Bricks Without Straw', *Vogue*, December 1979, p.108.
10. Polly Devlin, 'Polly Devlin on Jean Rhys', *Vogue*, December 1979, p.114.
11. Francis Wyndham and Diana Melly, eds, *Jean Rhys Letters, 1931–1966* (London: André Deutsch, 1984) p.187.
12. Ibid., p.171.
13. In the same letter, Rhys denies that *Quartet* was 'autobiography'.
14. Kate Millett, *Sexual Politics* (London: Hart-Davis, 1969) p.194. See also: pp.194–7, 203, 204–6.
15. In *Tigers Are Better-Looking* (Harmondsworth: Penguin, 1972) pp.162–5.
16. See: Andrea Dworkin, *Woman Hating* (New York: Dutton, 1974), and *Our Blood: Prophecies and Discoveries on Sexual Politics* (London: The Women's Press, 1982).
17. *Our Blood*, pp.11–12.
18. 'I'm not at all for women's lib.' Jean Rhys quoted in David Plante, *Difficult Women* (London: Gollancz, 1983) p.40.
19. *Our Blood*, p.47.
20. *Woman Hating*, pp.47–9.
21. Gérard Genette, *Narrative Discourse* (Oxford: Blackwell, 1980).

CHAPTER 1: REDUCING FIFI

1. *The Left Bank* (London: Jonathan Cape, 1927).
2. 'Frequently lacking in subtlety or depth, the stories nevertheless

contain in embryo the themes and ideas which will dominate Rhys's novels.' Staley, p.20.

3. Diegesis (story): This is 'the signified or narrative content (even if this content turns out, in a given case, to be low in dramatic intensity or fullness of incident)' of the discourse. *Narrative Discourse*, p.27.

4. In *Tigers Are Better-Looking*, p.173. All page references to the stories from *The Left Bank* will be to the Penguin edition of *Tigers Are Better-Looking* (Harmondsworth, 1972).

5. Free indirect style: This is where 'the narrator takes on the speech of the character, or ... the character speaks through the voice of the narrator, and the two instances are *merged.*' *Narrative Discourse*, p.174.

6. *Narrative Discourse*, pp.184–5.

7. Ibid., p.185.

8. *Tigers are Better-Looking*, p.176.

9. Analepsis (retrospection): 'Any evocation after the fact of an event that took place earlier than the point in the story where we are at any given moment.' *Narrative Discourse*, p.40.

10. *Narrative Discourse*, p.185.

CHAPTER 2: MARYA'S IRONY

1. Meriel McCooey, 'The Passionate Victim: Jean Ivory's film "Quartet" ... by Jean Rhys.', *The Sunday Times Magazine*, 14 June 1981, p.30.

2. Staley, p.37.

3. pp.7–14. All my references to the texts of Jean Rhys will be to the Penguin editions.

4. See Roland Barthes, *S/Z*, trans. Richard Miller (New York: Hill and Wang, 1974). Any statement which is 'made in a collective and anonymous voice originating in traditional human experience' conforms to the cultural code. These statements may be 'references to a science or body of knowledge'. *S/Z*, pp.18–20.

5. Iterative narrative: 'Narrating one time (or rather: at one time) what happened *n* times.' *Narrative Discourse*, p.116.

6. Singulative narrative: 'Narrating once what happened once.' *Narrative Discourse*, p.114.

7. *Quartet*, p.8.

8. Ibid., p.10.

9. Prolepsis (anticipation): 'Any narrative manoeuvre that consists of narrating or evoking in advance an event that will take place later.' *Narrative Discourse*, p.40.

CHAPTER 3: JULIA AND THE 'OTHERS'

1. *After Leaving Mr Mackenzie* (Harmondsworth: Penguin, 1971) p.27.

2. Ibid., p.48.

3. '... Why should you look at me suspiciously, as if I were one of the

others? I'm not one of the others; I'm on your side. Can't you see that? I'm for you and for people like you, and I'm against the others.' *After Leaving Mr Mackenzie*, p.121.

4. Following her mother's death, Norah confides to Julia that she intends to leave London and that Wyatt will accompany her. *After Leaving Mr Mackenzie*, pp.96–7.

CHAPTER 4: ANNA'S DARKNESS

1. The name 'Nana' has been used in a more recent work on prostitution, that of Jean Luc Godard's *Vivre Sa Vie*, in which the main character bears exactly the same name as Zola's heroine.

2. Vincent asks: '"What in God's name were you doing on the pier at Southsea?" Walter blinked. Then he said, "You shouldn't let Vincent pump you ..."'. *Voyage in the Dark* (Harmondsworth: Penguin, 1969) p.74.

3. This sort of departure into memory is one of twenty such occurrences in the text. Together, they weave a rich tapestry throughout the novel, and by doing so develop the idea of a contrast between an exotic past enjoyed by the narrator, and the dull reality of the present. Moreover, they provide us with a vivid insight into the narrator's background, showing her in her years of development from childhood to adolescence, and accounting, in part, for the difficulties which she experiences in adjusting to her new way of life. See *Voyage in the Dark*: pp.7, 15, 27–8, 36–8, 44–9, 58–63, 67, 71, 77–8, 79–81, 83, 84, 91, 107, 115, 127, 128–30, 138–41, 151, 156–8.

4. See Louis James, p.34.

5. *The Tempest* (Act V, Sc. I): Miranda's words are: 'O, wonder! / How many goodly creatures are there here! / How beauteous mankind is! / O brave new world, / That has such people in't!' They are tempered by Prospero's comment: ''Tis new to thee.'

6. Cf. effect of the first sentence of the novel: 'It was as if a curtain had fallen, hiding everything I had ever known.' *Voyage in the Dark*, p.7.

7. Ibid., pp.31–4.

8. Ibid., pp.28–9.

9. Ibid., p.26.

10. See Jacqueline Rose's introduction to *Feminine Sexuality: Jacques Lacan and the École Freudienne* (London: Macmillan, 1983) pp.30–3.

11. Flaubert, *Madame Bovary* (Paris: Gallimard, 1972) p.432.

12. *Voyage in the Dark*, p.81.

13. *Progression d'effet*: 'In writing a novel we agreed that every word set on paper ... must carry the story forward and, that as the story progressed, the story must be carried forward faster and faster with more and more intensity.' Ford Madox Ford in: Frank MacShane, ed., *Critical Writings of Ford Madox Ford* (Lincoln: University of Nebraska Press, 1964) p.87.

14. Anna responds comparatively coolly on hearing the contents of the letter of complaint about her which Matthews writes to Laurie. See *Voyage in the Dark*, p.143.

15. See *Voyage in the Dark*, pp.112–13; and a discussion of the significance of the décor, in Louis James, p.35.
16. Ethel herself confirms this later in a letter of complaint which she writes to Laurie: 'A picture I had – the glass all smashed and there is the picture without a glass . . .', p.142.

CHAPTER 5: SASHA IN NARRATIVE CONTROL

1. Autodiegetic narrative: In this, the narrator is 'the hero of the story he tells', not a mere 'observer' or 'witness'. *Narrative Discourse*, p.245.
2. 'I can see Sidonie carefully looking round for an hotel just like this one.', *Good Morning, Midnight* (Harmondsworth: Penguin, 1969) p.12.
3. Sasha tells Delmar that she arrived in Paris just after the war (p.56). A little later in the diegesis, she locates the time of the diegesis on the first narrative level: 'This is late October, 1937', (p.76).
4. He tells Sasha: 'Remember – that evening I met you. I was discouraged, very discouraged. You brought me luck.' *Good Morning, Midnight*, p.127.
5. This theme is also touched on elsewhere in the novel: 'When you are dead to the world, the world often rescues you, if only to make a figure of fun out of you.' (p.76); '. . . once again I have given damnable human beings the right to pity me and laugh at me.' (p.78); 'We are reading *Lady Windermere's Fan*. "The laughter, the horrible laughter of the world – a thing more tragic than all the tears the world has ever shed. . . ."' (p.115).

CHAPTER 6: ANTOINETTE AND EDWARD: LOCATING THE TRAGIC FIGURE

1. This is Mrs Eff's description of the younger Rochester. *Wide Sargasso Sea* (Harmondsworth: Penguin, 1968) p.145.
2. This attitude is demonstrated in *Quartet*. See *Quartet*, p.64.
3. *Letters*, p.271.
4. 'Antoinette had a room to herself . . .'. *Wide Sargasso Sea*, p.58.
5. Amélie tells Edward that Daniel is 'a very superior man, always reading the Bible' and that 'one time he was a preacher in Barbados'. *Wide Sargasso Sea*, pp.99–100.
6. See *Wide Sargasso Sea*, p.97.
7. Edward is the narrator in this case.
8. *Wide Sargasso Sea*, pp.135–6.
9. 'It was a beautiful place – wild, untouched, above all untouched, with an alien, disturbing, secret loveliness. And it kept its secret. I'd find myself thinking, "What I see is nothing – I want what it *hides* – that is not nothing."' *Wide Sargasso Sea*, p.73.
10. *Macbeth* i, vii, 21–2.

Index